A-Z SLOUGH an

CW00722237

CONTENT

Key to Map Pages	2-3
Map Pages	4-25
Index	... onwards

REFERENCE

Motorway	M4
A Road	A332
B Road	B3022
Dual Carriageway	
One-way Street Traffic flow on A roads is indicated by a heavy line on the drivers' left.	➡
Junction Names	LANGLEY ROUNDABOUT
Restricted Access	
Pedestrianized Road	
Track & Footpath	
Residential Walkway	
Railway	Station / Level Crossing / Tunnel
Built-up Area	HIGH ST.
Local Authority Boundary	
Posttown Boundary	
Postcode Boundary (within posttown)	
Map Continuation	12

Car Park (selected)	P
Church or Chapel	†
Fire Station	■
Hospital	H
House Numbers (A & B Roads only)	2 / 33
Information Centre	i
National Grid Reference	500
Park & Ride	Windsor (Home Park) P+
Police Station	▲
Post Office	★
Toilet: without facilities for the Disabled with facilities for the Disabled Disabled facilities only	
Educational Establishment	
Hospital or Hospice	
Industrial Building	
Leisure or Recreational Facility	
Place of Interest	
Public Building	
Shopping Centre or Market	
Other Selected Buildings	

Scale 1:19,000
3⅓ inches (8.47 cm) to 1 mile
5.26 cm to 1 kilometre

0 — ¼ — ½ — ¾ Mile
0 — 250 — 500 — 750 Metres — 1 Kilometre

Copyright of Geographers' A-Z Map Company Limited

Fairfield Road, Borough Green, Sevenoaks, Kent TN15 8PP
Telephone: 01732 781000 (Enquiries & Trade Sales)
01732 783422 (Retail Sales)

www.a-zmaps.co.uk

Copyright © Geographers' A-Z Map Co. Ltd.

Ordnance Survey® This product includes mapping data licensed from Ordnance Survey® with the permission of the Controller of Her Majesty's Stationery Office.

© Crown Copyright 2005. All rights reserved. Licence number 100017302

EDITION 4 2006

Every possible care has been taken to ensure that, to the best of our knowledge, the information contained in this atlas is accurate at the date of publication. However, we cannot warrant that our work is entirely error free and whilst we would be grateful to learn of any inaccuracies, we do not accept any responsibility for loss or damage resulting from reliance on information contained within this publication.

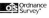

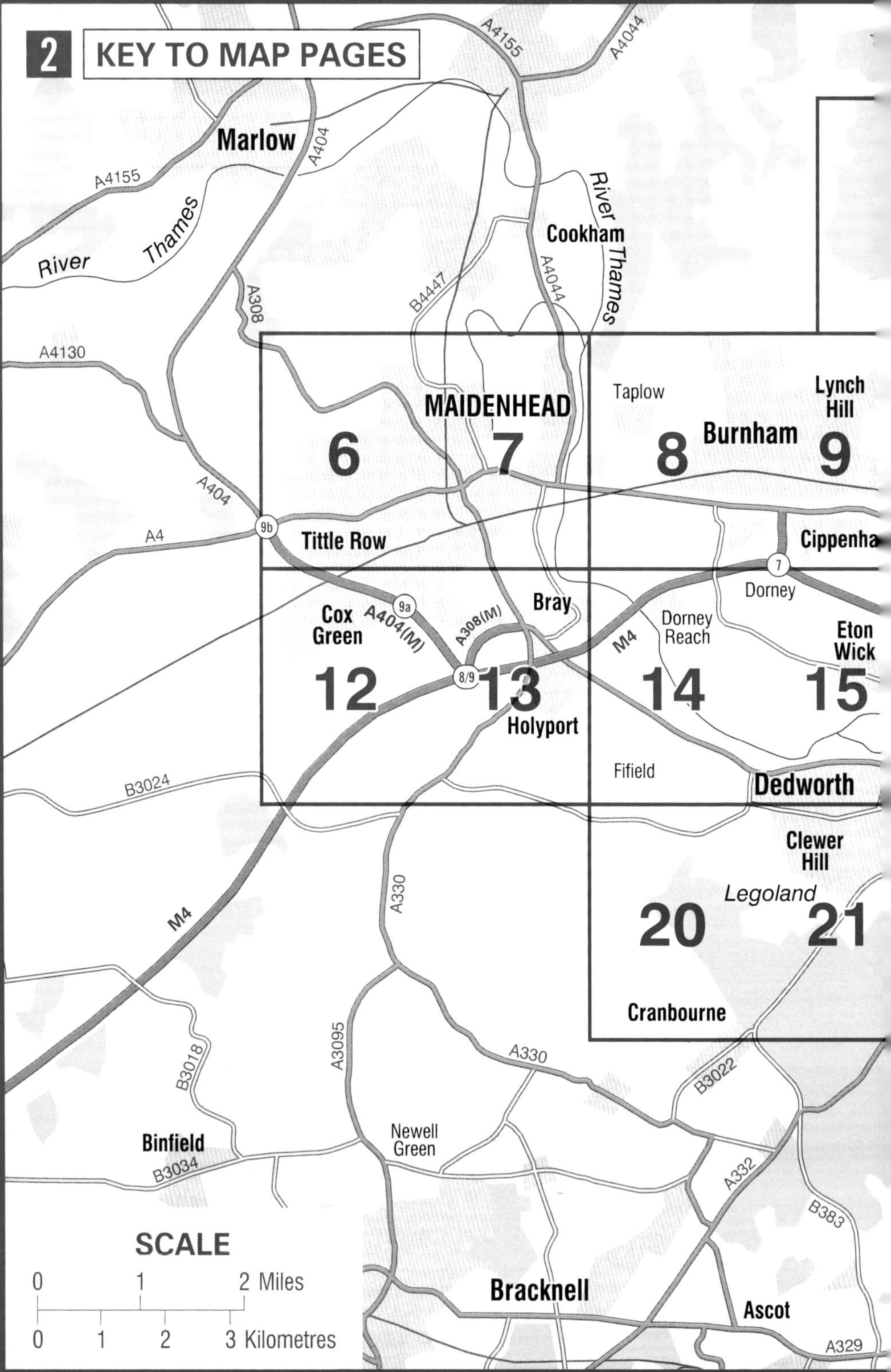
2
KEY TO MAP PAGES
A4155
A4044
Marlow
A404
A4155
River Thames
River Thames
Cookham
A4044
B4447
A308
A4130
MAIDENHEAD
Taplow
Lynch Hill
Burnham
6
7
8
9
A404
9b
A4
Tittle Row
Cippenha
7
Dorney
Cox Green
9a
A404(M)
A308(M)
Bray
M4
Dorney Reach
Eton Wick
8/9
12
13
14
15
Holyport
Fifield
B3024
Dedworth
Clewer Hill
A330
Legoland
20
21
M4
Cranbourne
A3095
A330
B3018
B3022
Binfield
Newell Green
B3034
A332
B383
SCALE
0 1 2 Miles
0 1 2 3 Kilometres
Bracknell
Ascot
A329

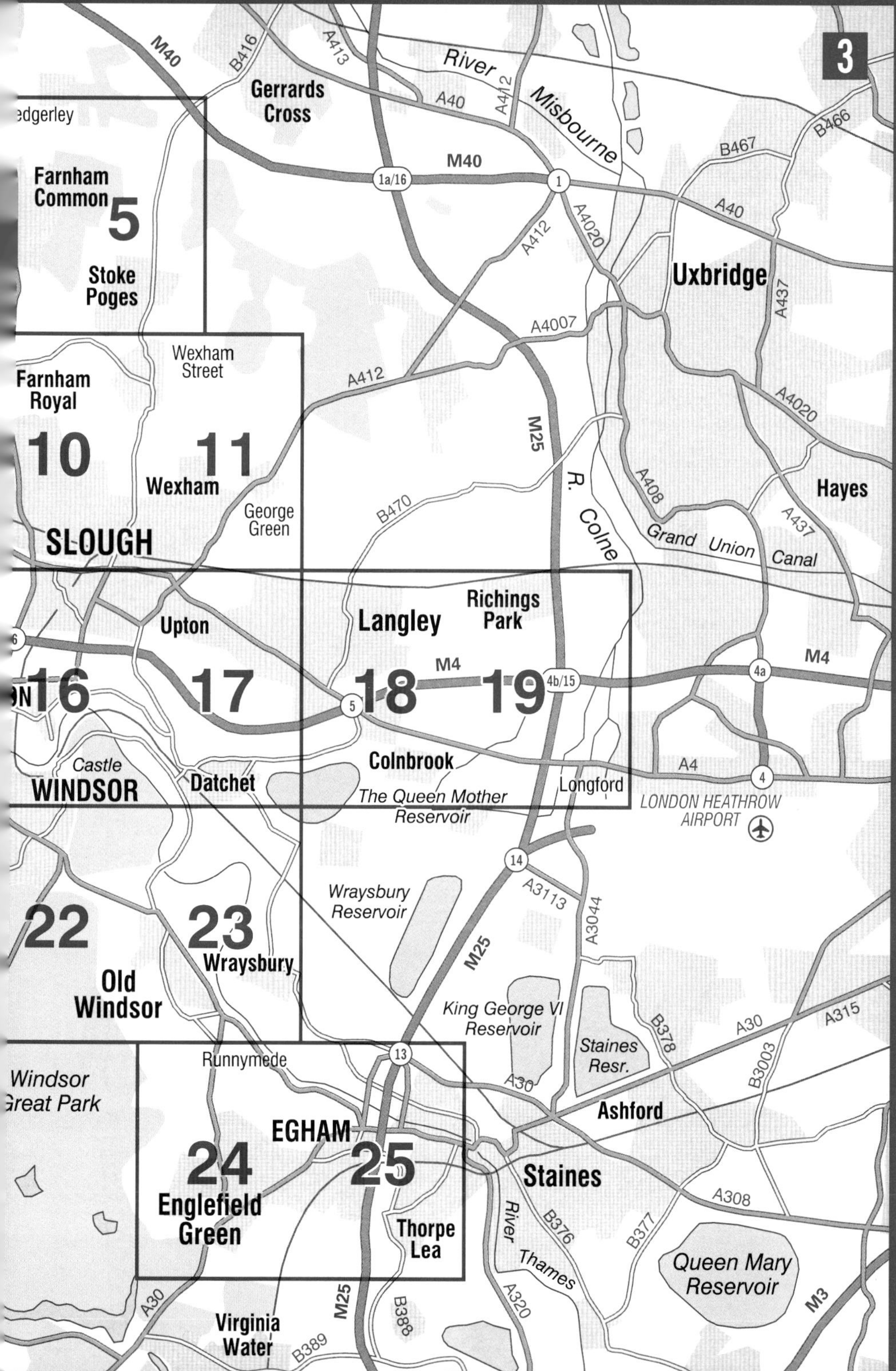
M40
B416
A413
Gerrards
Cross
River Misbourne
A412
A40
M40
1a/16
1
A4020
A412
A40
B466
B467
Uxbridge
A437
A4007
A412
edgerley
Farnham
Common
5
Stoke
Poges
Wexham
Street
Farnham
Royal
10
11
Wexham
George
Green
SLOUGH
B470
M25
R. Colne
A408
A4020
A437
Hayes
Grand Union Canal
Langley
Richings
Park
Upton
M4
M4
16
17
18
19
4b/15
4a
5
6
Castle
WINDSOR
Datchet
Colnbrook
The Queen Mother
Reservoir
Longford
A4
4
LONDON HEATHROW
AIRPORT
14
A3113
A3044
Wraysbury
Reservoir
22
23
Wraysbury
M25
Old
Windsor
King George VI
Reservoir
Staines
Resr.
B378
A30
A315
B3003
Runnymede
13
A30
Windsor
Great Park
EGHAM
Ashford
24
25
Englefield
Green
Staines
A308
Thorpe
Lea
River Thames
B376
B377
Queen Mary
Reservoir
M3
A30
M25
B388
A320
Virginia
Water
B389

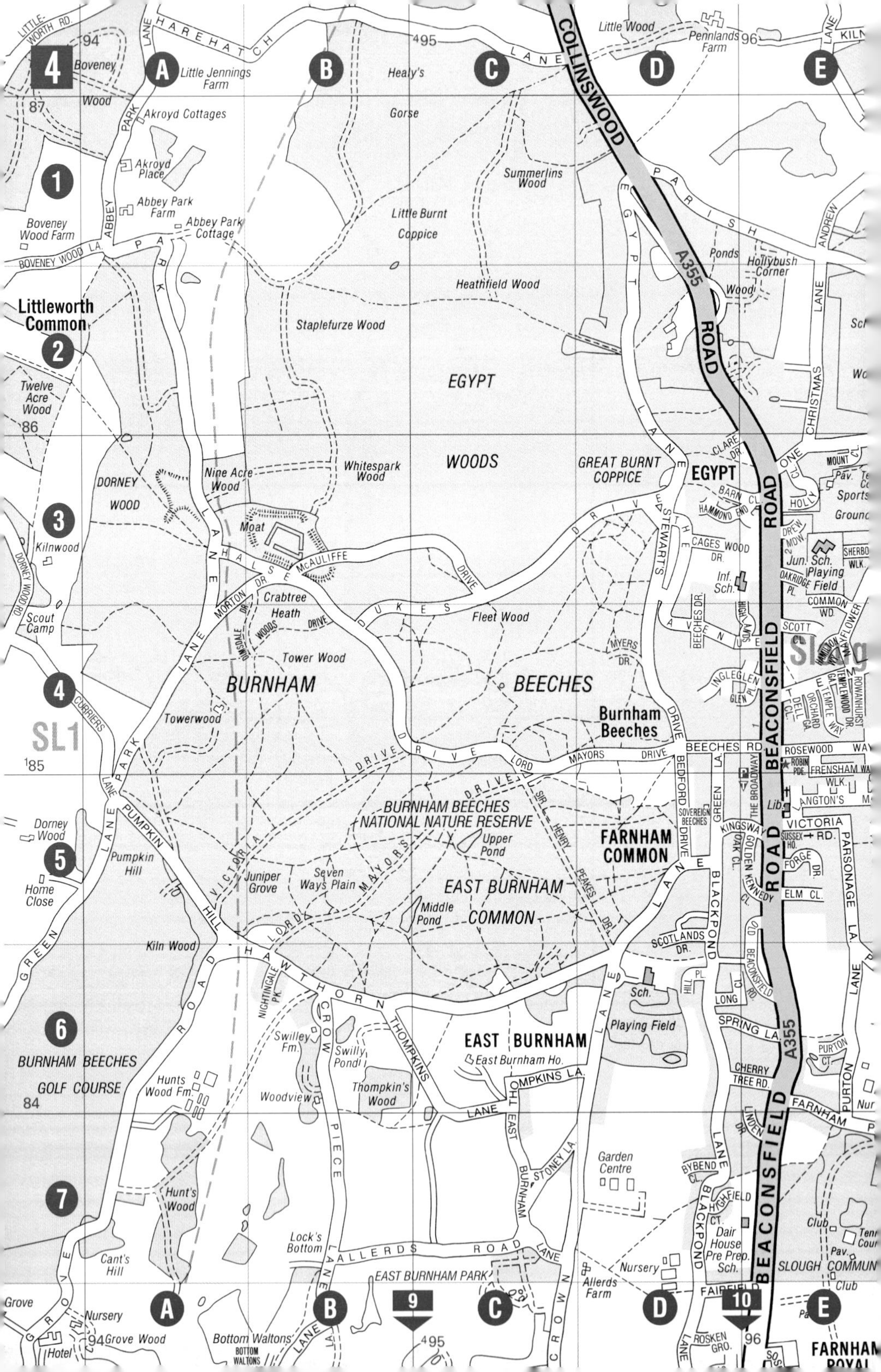
LITTLEWORTH RD.
HAREHATCH LANE
COLLINSWOOD ROAD
Little Wood
Pennlands Farm
Boveney Wood
Little Jennings Farm
Healy's Gorse
Akroyd Cottages
Akroyd Place
Abbey Park Farm
Abbey Park Cottage
ABBEY PARK
Boveney Wood Farm
BOVENEY WOOD LA.
Summerlins Wood
Little Burnt Coppice
Heathfield Wood
PARISH LANE
A355
Ponds
Hollybush Corner
Wood
ANDREW
CHRISTMAS LANE
Littleworth Common
Staplefurze Wood
EGYPT WOODS
EGYPT LANE
BEACONSFIELD ROAD
Twelve Acre Wood
DORNEY WOOD
Nine Acre Wood
Whitespark Wood
GREAT BURNT COPPICE
EGYPT
CLARE DR.
BARN CL.
HAMMOND END
HOLLY CL.
MOUNT CL.
Pav.
Sports Ground
Kilnwood
DORNEY WOOD RD.
Moat
HALSE DRIVE
McAULIFFE DRIVE
STEWARTS DRIVE
CAGES WOOD DR.
DREW MDW.
Jun. Sch.
Playing Field
Inf. Sch.
OAKRIDGE PL.
COMMON WD.
Scout Camp
MORTON DR.
DUKES DRIVE
Crabtree Heath
DIMSDALE DR.
WOODS DRIVE
Fleet Wood
BEECHES DR.
AVENUE
HIGH MDW.
SCOTT CL.
Tower Wood
MYERS DR.
Slough
BURNHAM BEECHES
INGLEGLEN
GLEN PL.
TEMPLEWOOD
ROWANHURST DR.
ORCHARD
TEMPLE WAY
DELL CL.
MAYFLOWER
HAMILTON PK.
Towerwood
SL1
CURRIERS
PARK LANE
Burnham Beeches
LORD MAYORS DRIVE
BEECHES RD.
BEDFORD DRIVE
ROSEWOOD WAY
ROBIN PDE.
FRENSHAM WALK
THE BROADWAY
GREEN LA.
LANGTON'S
Lib.
BURNHAM BEECHES NATIONAL NATURE RESERVE
SIR HENRY PEAKES DR.
Dorney Wood
VICTORIA DRIVE
Upper Pond
FARNHAM COMMON
SOVEREIGN BEECHES
KINGSWAY
OAK CL.
GOLDEN KENNEDY CL.
VICTORIA RD.
SUSSEX HO.
FORGE DR.
PARSONAGE LA.
Home Close
Pumpkin Hill
PUMPKIN HILL
Juniper Grove
Seven Ways Plain
EAST BURNHAM COMMON
ELM CL.
Middle Pond
BLACKPOND LANE
OLD BEACONSFIELD RD.
SCOTLANDS DR.
Kiln Wood
HAWTHORN LANE
NIGHTINGALE PK.
HILL PL.
LONG CL.
Sch.
Playing Field
SPRING LA.
GREEN LANE
BURNHAM BEECHES GOLF COURSE
Swilley Fm.
Swilly Pond
CROW PIECE LANE
THOMPKINS LANE
EAST BURNHAM
East Burnham Ho.
THOMPKINS LA.
PURTON CT.
PURTON LANE
CHERRY TREE RD.
Hunts Wood Fm.
Woodview
Thompkin's Wood
FARNHAM
LINDEN DR.
Nur
EAST BURNHAM LANE
STONEY LA.
Garden Centre
BYBEND CL.
HIGHFIELD CT.
Hunt's Wood
Dair House Pre Prep. Sch.
Club
Pav.
Tennis Courts
Lock's Bottom
ALLERDS ROAD
Cant's Hill
EAST BURNHAM PARK
Allerds Farm
Nursery
SLOUGH COMMUNITY
CROWN LANE
FAIRFIELD
GROVE
Grove
Nursery
Grove Wood
Hotel
Bottom Waltons
BOTTOM WALTONS
9
10
ROSKEN GRO.
FARNHAM ROYAL
A B C D E
1 2 3 4 5 6 7
94 87 86 85 84 495 96

5
F
G
H
J
K
97
98
99
Court Farm
Ten. Ct.
Church Wood Reserve
CHILTERN
HEDGERLEY
Hanging Wood
Hedgerley Hill
STEVENSON RD.
JONES WAY
ELKINS RD.
WOOD LA.
COPPICE WAY
GREGORY ROAD
ROBERT RD.
COTTAGE PARK RD.
HEDGERLEY
LONGFIELD
Black Grove
The Pin Farm
Reservoir (Covered)
HEDGERLEY PARK
Park House
HILL LANE
Tara
HUNDREDS
Hedgerley Park Farm
COLLUM GREEN ROAD
TIMBER WOOD
WOOD END CL.
HEATHERSIDE GDS.
ROMSEY DR.
TIMBER WOOD
Reservoir (covered)
Stoke Wood
GYPSY LANE
COLLEY WOOD
STOKE WOOD
Piggery
Templemead
ASHENDEN WLK.
SL2
WOOD LANE
GRANGE GS.
Gerrards Cross
M40 MOTORWAY
MOUNT HILL LANE
Mount Hill Farm
High Meadows
WINDSOR RD.
DUKES KILN DR.
DUKES VALLEY
Mounthill Wood
M40
SL9
Duke's Orchard
Riding Stables
B416
Pickeridge Wood
Parkside Cemetery
WINDSOR ROAD
1
2
3
4
5
6
7
87
86
185
84
Pickeridge Farm
Kestrel Farm
SL3
Stoke Common
STOKE COMMON ROAD
LARCHMOOR PARK
STOKE COMMON
Duffield Fm.
DUFFIELD LANE
GERRARDS CROSS ROAD
Frame Wood
VINE ROAD
VINE WAY
FIRCROFT CL.
NEVILLE CL.
ASHURST CL.
CLEVEHURST CL.
ELDERFIELD RD.
WAKEFIELD CR.
FREEMANS CLOSE
Brockhurst Wood
RICKMAN'S LANE
Heath
Wood
Copse
Brockhurst Wood
HAZELL
PENNYLETS GREEN
BUNBY RD.
HILL GRN.
BELLS
Liby.
BROOM HILL
HOLLYBUSH HILL
SEFTON PADDOCK
CHERRY ORCHARD
Eight Acres
Woodlands
Home Wood
Stoke Park
Old Orchard Wood
Old Orchard Ho.
Stoke Court
ASH GR.
ROGERS LANE
BOLD'S CT.
Sch.
WILLOW PK.
SEFTON PARK
Tennis Court
Home Farm
SCHOOL LANE
HOCKLEY LANE
Sch.
CHAPEL LA.
Little Orchard
AKESIDE DR.
DRIVE
STOKE COURT
GLENFIELDS
SEFTON CL.
Rec. Grd.
Pav.
Sports Grd.
Tennis Courts
DECIES WAY
BELLS HILL
Hockley Hole
HOME FARM WAY
WEXHAM STREET
Rec. Grd.
LARKINGS LA.
TUBWELL RD.
DEANS CL.
FARNHAM PARK GOLF COURSE
Yew Place
LANE
STOKE
WEST END LANE
END CT.
ELIZABETH WAY
STOKE POGES
PENN MEADOW
HASTINGS MDW.
GREEN
PLOUGH LA.
PLOUGH LA.
THE THAMES VALLEY NUFFIELD HOSP.
WEXHAM STREET
Club House
Club Ho.
Tithe Fm.
10
11
PARK ROAD
B416
GRAYS PARK RD.
FARTHING
WEXHAM PARK GOLF COURSE
WEXHAM

A
B
C
D
E
86
87
1
2
3
4
5
6
7
83
82
81
180
Goulding's Wood
Park Corner
Harding's Grove
Beeching-grove Wood
Reservoir (Covered)
Herons Court
Works
Cannon Court Farm
Hindhay Farm
Shepherd Standing
Compton Elms
Lee Farm
Greenacre
Enmore
Ditton Meads
Ditton House
Pinkneys Farm
St. Timothee
The Orchards
Pinkneys Court
Pinkneys Green
Fernhurst
Rashleighs
Pav.
Cricket Ground
FURZE PLATT
Furze Platt Sch.
Playing Field
Furze Platt Jun. & Inf. Schs.
Recreation Ground
Bowling Green
Tennis Courts
Schools
Rec. Grd.
Maidenhead
Cemetery
ST. MARK'S HOSP.
Playing Field
Ten. Cts.
School
Playing Field
HIGHWAY
Punt Hill
Ckt. Ground
Maidenhead Thicket
Junction 9b
A404(M)
TITTLE ROW
Playing Field
Tennis Courts
Schs.
Thtre.
Sch.
Schs.
College
BOYN HILL
WOOLLEY GREEN
Ridgeway Sch.
Woolley Cottage
VANWALL BUSINESS PARK
Desborough Park
Ten. Cts.
12
MARLOW ROAD A308
FURZE
GOLDEN BALL LA.
MALDERS LANE
HINDHAY
WINTER HILL ROAD
PLATT A308
ROAD
LEE LANE
DARLING'S LANE
PINKNEYS DRIVE
CAMLEY PARK DR.
MOORLANDS DRIVE
BIX LANE
BAKERS LA.
HENLEY ROAD
A404
BATH A4 RD.
BATH A4 ROAD
CANNON LANE
ALTWOOD ROAD
A404(M) MOTORWAY
FARMERS WAY
CANNON COURT RD.
NIGHTINGALE LANE
SWITCHBACK RD.
ST. PETER'S RD.
MALVERN
LINDEN AV.
BELMONT PARK AV.
GROVE
ST. MARK'S ROAD
ST. MARK'S CRESCENT
COURTHOUSE ROAD
ALL SAINTS AVENUE
CROMWELL RD.
GORDON RD.
WELLINGTON RD.
COLLEGE RD.
RISELEY RD.
BOYN HILL AV.
BOYN VALLEY RD.
NORDEN RD.
WOOTTON WAY
WESTBOROUGH RD.
STAMFORD RD.
CLARE RD.
HALIFAX RD.
LINCOLN ROAD
SUNDERLAND RD.
BLENHEIM ROAD
ALLENBY RD.
OAKEN GROVE
CLAREFIELD DR.
CRANBROOK DR.
BALMORAL
MALLOW PK.
DORCHESTER CL.
LYNEHAM GDS.
GWENDALE
HEMSDALE
AVONDALE
BRAMPTON DR.
WINSTON CT.
LANCASTER RD.
HEADINGTON RD.
GREEN LANE
FARM ROAD
HIGHWAY ROAD
HIGHWAY AVENUE
MARLBOROUGH RD.
MARLBOROUGH CL.
NAPIER ROAD
WESTFIELD RD.
WAVELL RD.
BIRDWOOD RD.
TWYNHAM RD.
HAVELOCK RD.
HAVELOCK CRES.
PORTLOCK RD.
POWNEY RD.
ORCHARD GR.
STONEFIELD PK.
PENYSTON RD.
TALBOTS DR.
SHERWOOD DR.
BEECHWOOD DR.
SILVER TREES DR.
SANDISPLATT RD.
AUDLEY DR.
BADMINTON RD.
GREAT HILL CRESCENT
CARISBROOKE CL.
SHIRLEY RD.
ALTWOOD DR.
ALTWOOD CL.
LEES CLOSE
LEES GDS.
BLOOMFIELD RD.
WEBSTER CLOSE
TIMBERS WLK.
GARDENS CLOSE
BANNARD RD.
TURPINS GRN.
BARLEY MEAD
THATCHERS DR.
PHEASANTS CROFT
COPTHORN CL.
CULLEY WAY
FURROW WAY
PAGET CL.
WELBY CL.
BRAMBLE LANE
VANWALL ROAD
VAUXHALL RD.
SILVERSTONE M.
NORREYS DR.
DESBOROUGH CR.
RIXMAN CL.
BRUNEL WAY
FANE WAY
LARCHFIELD RD.
CHAPEL ST.
SUFFOLK RD.
BEECHFIELD
KENNEDY CL.
BRAMLEY CHASE
ST. CHADS
ST. COLUMBUS
NORTHUMBRIA

F
G
H
J
K
89
490
MAIDENHEAD COURT
Sheephouse Farm
LOWER COOKHAM ROAD A4094
WHITEBROOK PARK
BATTLEMEAD CL.
ISLET PARK DRIVE
ISLET RD.
ISLET ROAD
THE AVENUE
EBSWORTH CL.
AMBERLEY CT.
COURT DR.
RIVER THAMES
WINDSOR & MAIDENHEAD
SOUTH BUCKS
83
CLIVEDEN MEAD
POPLARS GRO.
ASHLEY PARK
TUDOR CT.
LOCK AV.
BOULTERS LOCK ISLAND
Ray Mill Island
HORSHAM REACH
JUBILEE RIVER
Glen Island
Boat House
Taplow Court
Paper Mill
82
GARDNER RD.
COOKHAM ROAD
B4447
ALDEBURY RD.
PARTRIDGE MEAD
Cricket Ground
Sailing Club
Depot
SUMMERLEAZE RD.
LAKESIDE
BLACKAMOOR LANE
Summerleaze Lake
NORTH TOWN
Furze Platt
Nursy. Sch.
HARROW SCHOOL LA.
MOOR LANE
LAGGAN ROAD
MOORSIDE CL.
ELLINGTON PARK
BRIDLE CL.
RAY MILL RD. EAST
RAY MILL RD. WEST
RAY PARK AV.
Claires Ct. Sch.
LONGWORTH DR.
Ten. Ct.
FRANCES AV.
DEREK RD.
LEIGHTON GDS.
CAMPERDOWN
MAIDENHEAD
Schs.
CORDWALLIS PARK
GROSVENOR DR.
LOCKBRIDGE CT.
RAY MEAD ROAD A4094
Grass Eyot
Dunloe Lodge
Boat House
Bridge Eyot
Warehouse
Gas Works
Lansdowne Ho.
Old Ct.
CASTLE HILL A308
CRAUFURD RI.
MARLOW R.
Coll.
COLLEGE AV.
Kidwells Park
Tennis Cts.
Megabowl
Leisure Cen.
Law Cts.
The Moor
SAINT CLOUD WAY
BAD GODESBERG WAY
BRIDGE ROAD A4
MAIDENHEAD BRIDGE
BATH RD. A4
ELLINGTON RD.
Tennis Cts.
GUARDS CLUB RD.
TAPLOW QUAYS
RIVER RD.
FRASCATI WAY
HIGH ST.
KING ST.
Bus Depot
INDUSTRIAL ESTATE
Wks.
B3028
Factory
OLDFIELD RD.
OLDACRES
CHAUNTRY RD.
81
Orkney House
Amerden Ponds
Cine.
Leis. Cen.
Grenfell Park
GRENFELL PLACE
BELL STREET
Maidenhead Utd. FC
Maidenhead
KINGS GROVE IND. EST.
SILCO
Depot
BOYN VALLEY IND. EST.
Ind. Est.
Factory
Sewage Works
FISHERY
Sch.
Riverbank House
Red House
BRAYWICK ROAD A308
Desborough Sch.
Club Ho.
BROWNFIELD GARDENS
Playing Field
SHOPPENHANGERS ROAD
RUSHINGTON AVENUE
Rushington Copse
Braywick Sports Centre
Pav.
GREEN LANE
BRAY ROAD
B3028
FISHERY RD.
RIVER THAMES
CHURCH RD.
MAIDENHEAD GOLF COURSE
Playing Field
Playing Field
Golf Driving Range
BRAY WICK
Club House
Crkt. Ground
Headpile Eyot
180
Barge Farm
1
2
3
4
5
6
7
8
13

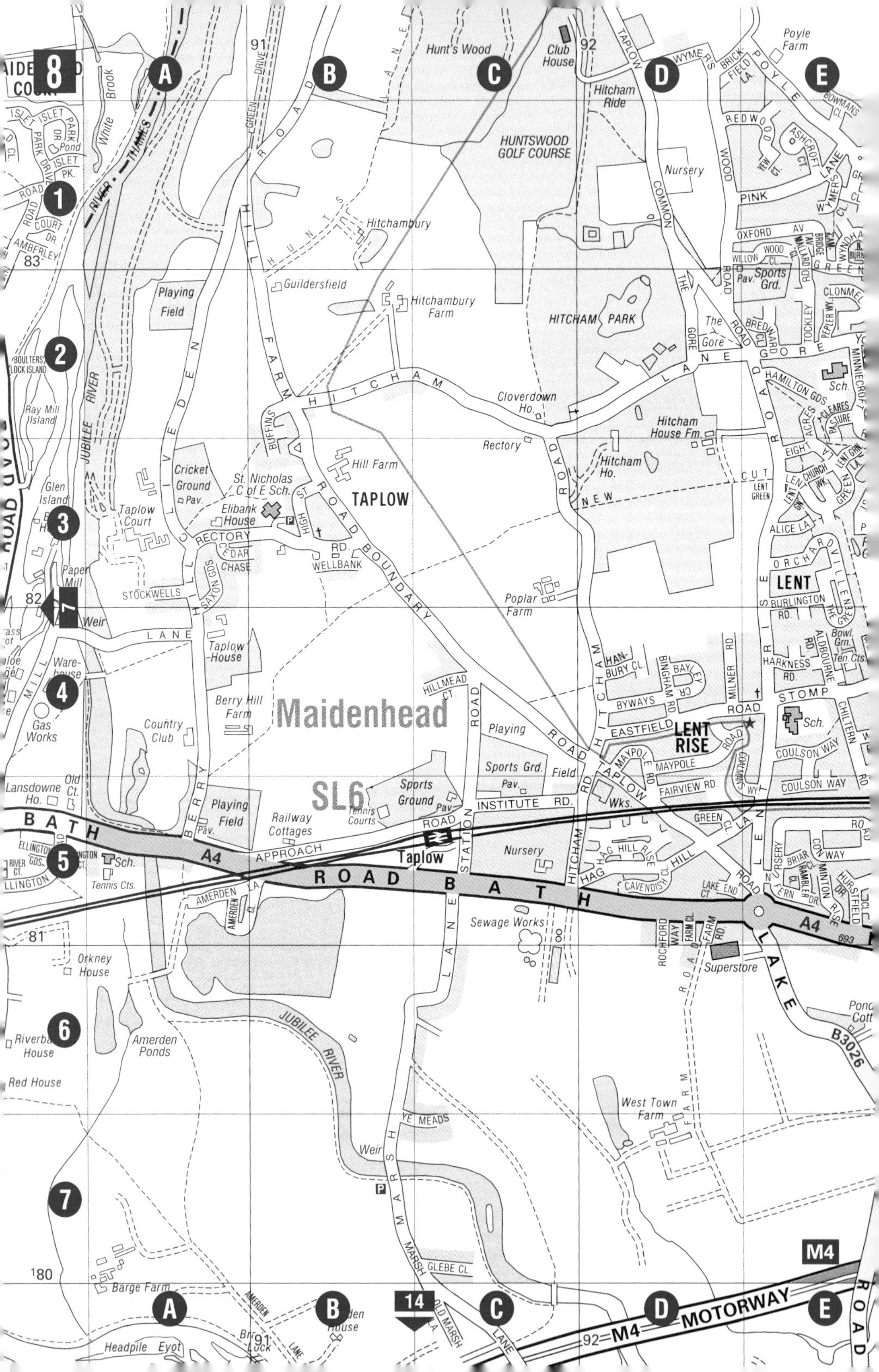

8
A
B
C
D
E
1
2
3
4
5
6
7
Hunt's Wood
Club House
Poyle Farm
Hitcham Ride
HUNTSWOOD GOLF COURSE
Nursery
White Brook
RIVER THAMES
Hitchambury
Guildersfield
Hitchambury Farm
Playing Field
HITCHAM PARK
The Gore
GORE ROAD
Cloverdown Ho.
Rectory
HITCHAM LANE
Hitcham House Fm.
Hitcham Ho.
NEW CUT
Boulters' Lock Island
Ray Mill Island
JUBILEE RIVER
Cricket Ground
Pav.
Taplow Court
St. Nicholas C of E Sch.
Elibank House
Hill Farm
TAPLOW
HIGH ST.
RECTORY RD.
CEDAR CHASE
WELLBANK
Glen Island
Paper Mill
Weir
STOCKWELLS
SAXON GDS.
LANE
Taplow House
Berry Hill Farm
Poplar Farm
BOUNDARY ROAD
LENT
LENT RISE
Ware-house
Gas Works
Country Club
Maidenhead
SL6
HILLMEAD CT.
Playing Field
Sports Grd.
Sports Ground
Tennis Courts
Railway Cottages
STATION ROAD
INSTITUTE RD.
HITCHAM RD.
TAPLOW RD.
EASTFIELD RD.
MAYPOLE RD.
FAIRVIEW RD.
Wks.
BYWAYS
BINGHAM RD.
BAYLEY CR.
MILNER RD.
STOMP ROAD
HANBURY CL.
Sch.
COULSON WAY
CHILTERN
HARKNESS RD.
ALDBOURNE RD.
Bowl. Grn.
Ten. Cts.
BURLINGTON RD.
ORCHARDVILLE
ALICE LA.
Lansdowne Ho.
Old Ct.
BATH ROAD
A4
APPROACH
Taplow
Nursery
HAG HILL RISE
CAVENDISH CL.
GREEN CL.
LAKE END CT.
LAKE END ROAD
Sewage Works
AMERDEN LA.
AMERDEN CL.
ROCHFORD WAY
FARM CL.
FARM RD.
Superstore
B3026
Pond Cott.
Orkney House
Riverbank House
Amerden Ponds
Red House
JUBILEE RIVER
West Town Farm
YE MEADS
Weir
MARSH LANE
GLEBE CL.
OLD MARSH LA.
Barge Farm
Headpile Eyot
Bray Lock
M4 MOTORWAY
M4
14
7
91
92
81
82
83
180
693
PINK LANE
OXFORD AV.
WILLOW CL.
Sports Grd.
REDWOOD
ASHCROFT CT.
BRICKFIELD LA.
WYMERS
BOWMANS CL.
TOCKLEY RD.
BREDWARD CL.
CLONMEL
HAMILTON GDS.
EIGHT ACRES
LENT GREEN
CHURCH WK.
BRIAR
CONWAY
NURSERY
FERN DR.
RAMBLER
HURSTFIELD DR.
MINTON RISE
ISLET PARK
AMBERLEY
COURT DR.
ELLINGTON
RIVER CT.
Tennis Cts.

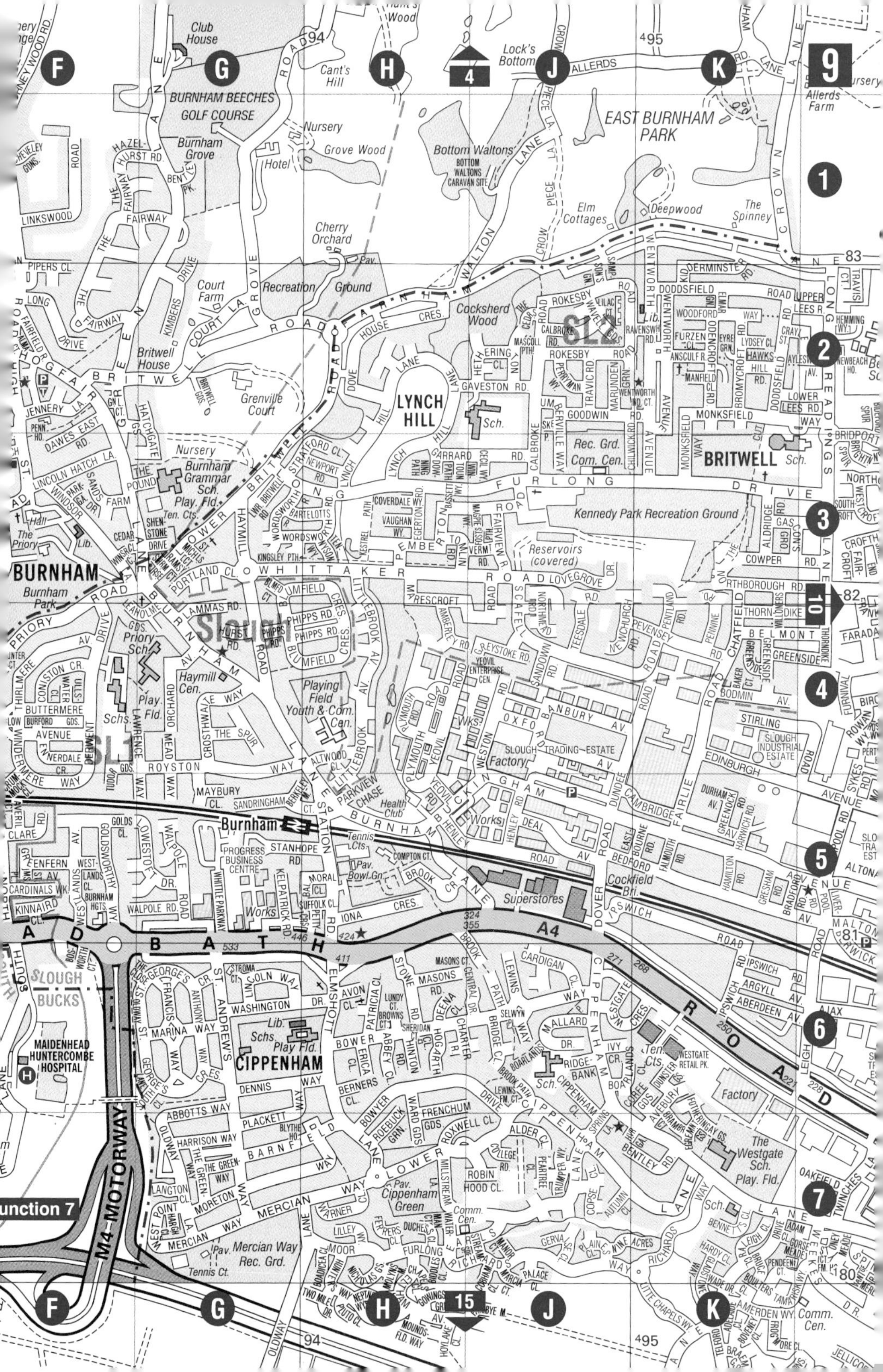

9
4
10
15
F
G
H
J
K
1
2
3
4
5
6
7
94
495
83
82
81
80
Club House
BURNHAM BEECHES GOLF COURSE
Burnham Grove
Cant's Hill
Lock's Bottom
ALLERDS RD.
EAST BURNHAM PARK
Allerds Farm
Nursery
Grove Wood
Hotel
Bottom Waltons
BOTTOM WALTONS CARAVAN SITE
Elm Cottages
Deepwood
The Spinney
CROWN LANE
PIECE LA.
WALTON LANE
Cherry Orchard
Pav.
Recreation Ground
Court Farm
Cocksherd Wood
FARNHAM ROAD
LINKSWOOD
PIPERS CL.
HAZELHURST RD.
THE FAIRWAY
FAIRWAY
KIMBERS DRIVE
GREEN LANE
COURT LA.
GROVE
BRITWELL ROAD
Britwell House
Grenville Court
LYNCH HILL
Sch.
SL2
KIDDERMINSTER RD.
DODDSFIELD ROAD
UPPER LEES R.
ROKESBY RD.
WENTWORTH AVENUE
RAVENSWOOD
Lib.
WOODFORD WAY
FURZEN CL.
LYDSEY CL.
HAWKS HILL RD.
ANSCULF R.
MANFIELD CL.
BROMYCROFT RD.
GAVESTON RD.
GOODWIN RD.
WENTWORTH IND. CT.
MONKSFIELD WAY
LOWER LEES RD.
Rec. Grd.
Com. Cen.
BRITWELL
Sch.
FURLONG DRIVE
GARRARD RD.
CALBROKE
STRATFORD CL.
NEWPORT RD.
Nursery
Burnham Grammar Sch.
Play. Fld.
Ten. Cts.
THE POUND
HATCHGATE
LINCOLN HATCH LA.
SANDS FARM
JENNERY LA.
DAWES EAST RD.
PENN. RD.
PARK-GATE DR.
WINDSOR
The Priory
Hall
Lib.
CEDAR
SHENSTONE DRIVE
BURNHAM
Burnham Park
PRIORY ROAD
LOWER BRITWELL
HAYMILL
WORDSWORTH
BARTELOTTS
COVERDALE WY.
VAUGHAN WY.
PEMBERTON RD.
FAIRVIEW R.
Kennedy Park Recreation Ground
Reservoirs (covered)
COWPER
ALDRIDGE
KINGSLEY PTH.
PORTLAND CL.
WHITTAKER ROAD
LOVEGROVE DR.
NORTHBOROUGH RD.
CHATFIELD
THORNDIKE
BELMONT
GREENSIDE
LAMMAS RD.
HURST RD.
Slough
PHIPPS RD.
BLUMFIELD CRES.
LITTLEBROOK AV.
MARESCROFT
AMBERLEY RD.
SCAFELL RD.
NORTHMEAD RD.
TEESDALE
NEWCHURCH RD.
PEVENSEY RD.
PENTLAND RD.
PENNINE RD.
GREYSTOKE RD.
YEOVIL ENTERPRISE CEN.
SANDOWN RD.
BANBURY AV.
OXFORD AV.
Priory Sch.
Haymill Cen.
Play. Fld.
Schs.
THIRLMERE AV.
CONISTON CR.
ULLSWATER
BUTTERMERE AVENUE
BURFORD GDS.
WINDERMERE WAY
ENNERDALE CR.
DERWENT DRIVE
SL1
LAWRENCE WAY
CROSTHWAITE WAY
THE SPUR
ORCHARD
MEAD WAY
ROYSTON WAY
TUDOR GDS.
MAYBURY CL.
Playing Field
Youth & Com. Cen.
ALTWOOD CL.
LITTLEBROOK
PARKVIEW CHASE
STATION RD.
PLYMOUTH RD.
YEOVIL RD.
WESTON RD.
Wks.
SLOUGH TRADING ESTATE
Factory
BUCKINGHAM AV.
DUNDEE RD.
CAMBRIDGE AV.
FAIRLIE RD.
BODMIN AV.
STIRLING RD.
SLOUGH INDUSTRIAL ESTATE
EDINBURGH AVENUE
DURHAM AV.
GREENOCK RD.
HARWICH RD.
SANDRINGHAM
Burnham
Health Club
BURNHAM LANE
Works
HENLEY RD.
DEAL AV.
EAST
BOURNE
FALMOUTH RD.
BEDFORD AV.
HAMILTON RD.
GRESHAM RD.
BRADFORD RD.
LIVERPOOL RD.
AVENUE
GOLDS CL.
LOWESTOFT DR.
WALPOLE RD.
CLARE RD.
FENFERN AV.
WESTLANDS AV.
CARDINALS WK.
KINNAIRD CL.
BURNHAM HGTS.
GOLDSWORTHY WY.
PROGRESS BUSINESS CENTRE
STANHOPE RD.
WHITTLE PARKWAY
KELPATRICK RD.
MORAL CL.
SUFFOLK CL.
Works
IONA CRES.
Tennis Cts.
COMPTON CT.
Pav. Bowl.Gn.
BROOK CR.
Superstores
Cockfield Bri.
DOVER ROAD
IPSWICH ROAD
BATH ROAD
A4
BROOK PATH
LEWINS WAY
CARDIGAN CL.
CIPPENHAM LANE
ARGYLL AV.
ABERDEEN AV.
AJAX
LEIGH RD.
SLOUGH
BUCKS
MAIDENHEAD HUNTERCOMBE HOSPITAL
ST. GEORGE'S CRES.
ST. FRANCIS
ST. ANDREW'S WAY
LINCOLN WAY
ANTHONY WAY
WASHINGTON DR.
ELMSHOT LANE
AVON CL.
PATRICIA CL.
STOWE RD.
MASONS RD.
MASONS CT.
DEENA CL.
CHARTER RD.
CENTRAL DR.
BRIDGE CL.
SELWYN PL.
MALLARD DR.
WESTGATE CRES.
IVY CR.
RIDGEBANK
Sch.
BOARLANDS CL.
Ten. Cts.
WESTGATE RETAIL PK.
Factory
MARINA WAY
Lib.
Schs.
Play Fld.
CIPPENHAM
BOWER WAY
ERICA CL.
ABBEY CL.
HINTON RD.
HOGARTH CL.
SHERIDAN CT.
LUNDY CT.
BROWNS CT.
DENNIS WAY
BERNERS CL.
ABBOTTS WAY
PLACKETT WAY
BLYTHE HO.
BOWYER DR.
ROEBUCK GRN.
WARD GDS.
FRENCHUM GDS.
ROXWELL CL.
ALDER CL.
COLLEGE RD.
PEARTREE CL.
TRUMPER WY.
SPRING LA.
BENTLEY RD.
CORFE GDS.
DUNSTER GDS.
AVEBURY
FOTHERINGAY GS.
The Westgate Sch.
Play. Fld.
OAKFIELD
TWINCHES LA.
HARRISON WAY
THE GREEN WAY
BARNFIELD
LOWER CIPPENHAM LANE
MILLSTREAM LA.
ROBIN HOOD CL.
COPSE CL.
AUTUMN CL.
LANGTON CL.
MORETON WAY
WEST POINT
MERCIAN WAY
LANE
Pav.
Cippenham Green
WARNER CL.
Comm. Cen.
LILLEY
FERRERS CL.
DUCHESS
FURLONG CL.
EARLS LA.
MOOR
Junction 7
M4 MOTORWAY
Pav.
Mercian Way Rec. Grd.
Tennis Ct.
BOADICEA CL.
NICHOLAS GS.
TWO MILE DR.
PLUTO CL.
NEPTUNE WAY
MOLYNS MEWS
CHAPELS
GONINGS
ST. RICHARDS
MARCIA CT.
PALACE CL.
GERVAISE CL.
PLAINES CL.
NINE ACRES
RICHARDS WAY
LITTLE CHAPELS WY.
Sch.
BENNETTS CL.
HARDY CL.
ADAM CL.
PENDEEN CT.
WEEKES DR.
AMERDEN WY.
Comm. Cen.
HOYLAKE CL.
MOUNDSFLD. WAY
OLDWAY LANE
TELFORD
JELLICOE

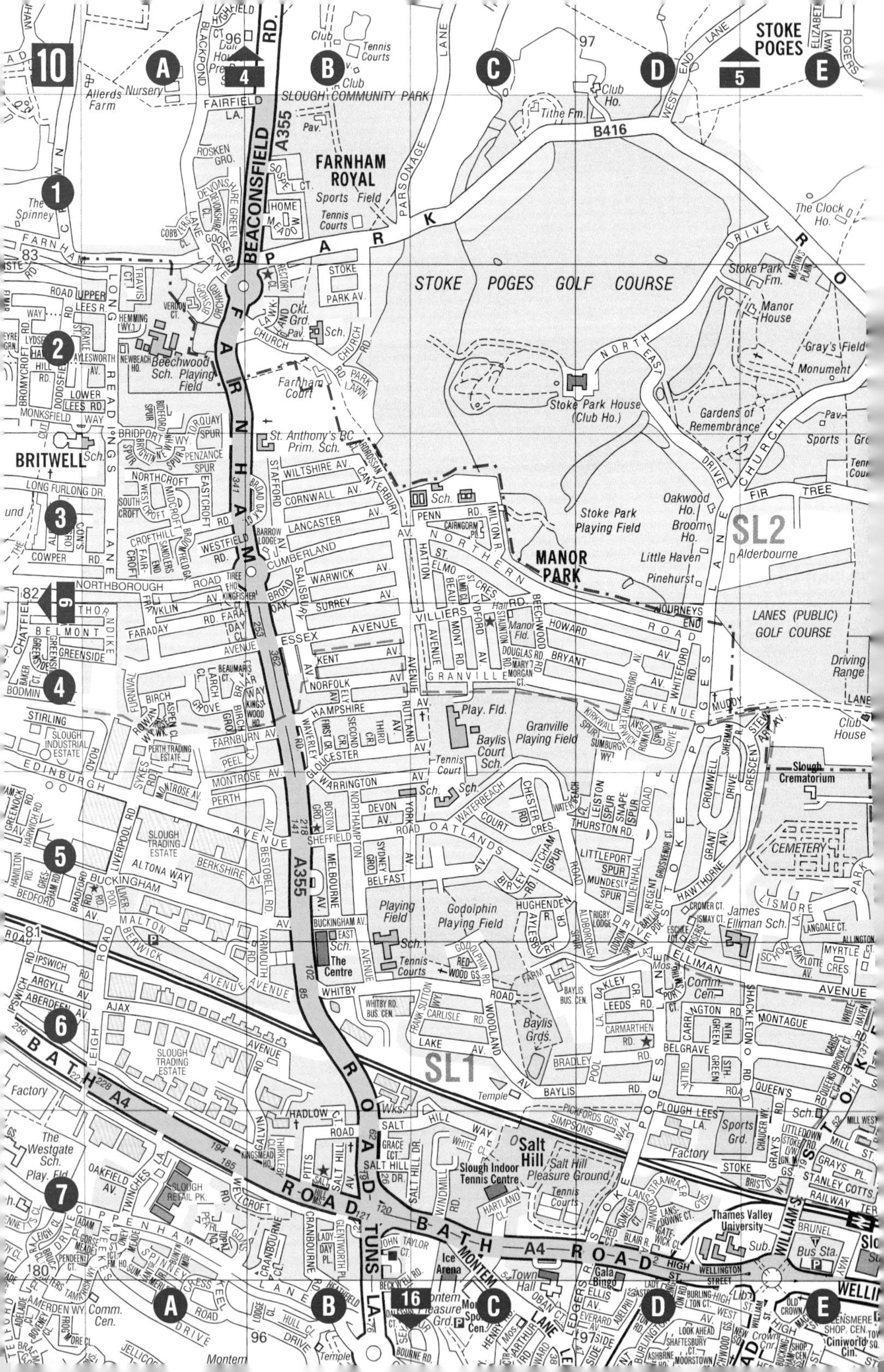

A
B
C
D
E
1
2
3
4
5
6
7
4
5
16
9
STOKE POGES
96
97
83
82
81
SLOUGH COMMUNITY PARK
FARNHAM ROYAL
Sports Field
Tennis Courts
Club
Allerds Farm
Nursery
The Spinney
FAIRFIELD LA.
ROSKEN GRO.
DEVONSHIRE GREEN
GOOSE GN.
BEACONSFIELD RD.
A355
B416
PARK RD.
FARNHAM LA.
FARNHAM RD.
Club Ho.
Tithe Fm.
WEST END LANE
PARSONAGE LANE
STOKE POGES GOLF COURSE
Stoke Park House (Club Ho.)
NORTH EAST DRIVE
Stoke Park Fm.
Manor House
Gray's Field
Monument
Gardens of Remembrance
Sports Grd.
The Clock Ho.
CHURCH RD.
FIR TREE
Oakwood Ho.
Broom Ho.
Little Haven
Pinehurst
Alderbourne
SL2
Stoke Park Playing Field
MANOR PARK
NORTHERN RD.
JOURNEYS END
HOWARD ROAD
LANES (PUBLIC) GOLF COURSE
Driving Range
Club House
Slough Crematorium
CEMETERY
STOKE POGES LANE
BRITWELL
Beechwood Sch. Playing Field
Farnham Court
St. Anthony's RC Prim. Sch.
WILTSHIRE AV.
CORNWALL AV.
LANCASTER AV.
CUMBERLAND AV.
WARWICK AV.
SURREY AV.
ESSEX AVENUE
KENT AV.
NORFOLK AV.
HAMPSHIRE AV.
GLOUCESTER AV.
NORTHBOROUGH ROAD
LONG READINGS LANE
LONG FURLONG DR.
COWPER RD.
FARADAY RD.
GREENSIDE
BELMONT
STIRLING
SLOUGH INDUSTRIAL ESTATE
EDINBURGH
PERTH TRADING ESTATE
FARNBURN AV.
MONTROSE AV.
PERTH AV.
SLOUGH TRADING ESTATE
ALTONA WAY
BERKSHIRE AV.
BUCKINGHAM AV.
LIVERPOOL RD.
Play. Fld.
Baylis Court Sch.
Granville Playing Field
GRANVILLE AVENUE
OATLANDS
Playing Field
Godolphin Playing Field
The Centre
Baylis Grds.
SL1
BAYLIS RD.
James Elliman Sch.
ELLIMAN AVENUE
MONTAGUE
Comm. Cen.
Salt Hill
Salt Hill Pleasure Ground
Slough Indoor Tennis Centre
BATH ROAD
A4
SLOUGH RETAIL PK.
The Westgate Sch. Play. Fld.
Factory
Thames Valley University
Bus Sta.
WELLINGTON STREET
Town Hall
Ice Arena
Montem Leisure Grd.
Gala Bingo
TUNS LA.
CIPPENHAM LANE
Comm. Cen.
Montem

F
G
H
J
K
5
17
1
2
3
4
5
6
7
THE THAMES VALLEY NUFFIELD HOSPITAL
Twin Trees Fm.
Sandhole Wood
Cuckoo Pen
ROWLEY LANE
BLACK PARK ROAD
WEXHAM STREET
War Mem.
Club House
WEXHAM PARK GOLF COURSE
Wexham Sports Centre
Rowley Wood
Rowleyfield Larches
Rowley Slip
Gallions Wood
Walk Wood
Blackpark Lake
Sawmill Cotts.
QUEEN'S DR.
Berry Farm
BUCKLAND GATE
Grotes Wood
Appletons
Spring Wood
Hollybush Wood
Pinewood Nurseries
Green Acres
Bell Fm.
Rowley Lake
Jubilee Plantation
Deodar Wood
B416 PARK ROAD
FARTHING GREEN LANE
PLOUGH LA.
TUBWELL R.
DEAN'S CL.
LARKINGS LA.
STOKE GREEN
Stoke Ho.
Park View
WEXHAM PARK HOSPITAL
GALLEONS LA.
STOKE GREEN
Stoke Place
Cricket Grd.
Pav.
CHURCH LANE
WEXHAM PARK LANE
Barry's Plantation
WILLIAM HARTLEY YD.
Wexham
Ten.Cts.
The Lodge
Play. Field
CHURCH GRO.
Wexham Sch.
Slough Supapitch
WEXHAM WOODS
GRANGE WOOD
WEXHAM PARK LA.
Stone's Wood
SL3
Langley Furze
Tennis Cts.
Bowl. Grn.
Play. Fld.
NORWAY DRIVE
LANGLEY PARK COUNTRY PARK
Driving Range
Slough Town FC (Wexham Park Stadium)
SOUTH BUCKS
SLOUGH
Slough
MANSEL CL.
BELL CL.
FARM CRES.
HILLERSDON
EDMUNDS WAY
MOAT DR.
Sch.
Wexham Court
OLD HOUSE CT.
LIDSTONE CT.
UXBRIDGE ROAD A412
RIXON CL.
CORONATION AV.
AUGUST END
KNOLTON WAY
THE CHERRIES
Playgrd
WINWOOD
BERRYFIELD
CHURCHFIELD M.
THE LINK
PRESTWOOD
NORMANS
QUINBROOKES
SHORT FERN
COFTARDS
DORNELS
MONTGOMERY PL.
DAWES MOOR CL.
POST OFFICE LA.
WOOD HOME
GEORGE GREEN RD.
WESTFIELD
THORN DR.
DIANA CL.
AZALEA WAY
ALAN WY.
MOREAU W.
GRAFTON CL.
GEORGE GREEN
MORAY DR.
BORDERSIDE
DUNBAR CL.
KOLA CT.
CLARENDON CT.
SHEEHY WY.
Tem.
FRITHE
HOLMEDALE
CANNON GA.
Masons Fm.
WITHYCROFT
Rec. Grd.
CALF LANE
GRASMERE
KENDAL DRIVE
AVENUE
UPTON LEA PDE.
MIRADOR CRES.
CARLTON
MAPLE CRES.
Rec. Grd.
PRESTON RD.
GLANMOR RD.
ELMWOOD RD.
BROADMARK RD.
HAZLEMERE ROAD
BERESFORD AV.
GRAND UNION CANAL
Play. Fld.
Schs.
MALPAS RD.
Comm. Cen.
ST. JOHNS RD.
GALLOWAY CHSE.
Islamic Cen.
CUMBRAE
AVENUE
ALBION CL.
WHITTENHAM
Works
Sub.
SLOUGH
THE BUSINESS VILLAGE
Gas Works
ROCHFORDS GARDENS
MEDLAR CT.
SERMED CT.
WARREN PDE.
Nursery
Home Farm
Convent of Our Lady Queen of Apostles
The Manor House
St. Paul's House
CROMWELLS COURT
PICKFORD DRIVE
ORCHRD WY.
FIRS DR.
Southend Farm
Grove Fm.
MIDDLE GREEN
MIDDLE GREEN
ST. MARY'S ROAD
ORCHARDS RESIDENTIAL PARK
Moat
Wildcroft
Lavender Farm
NURSERY LANE
MIDDLEGREEN
Langley Manor School
GOODMAN PARK
Recreation Ground
MARISH WHARF
MIDDLEGREEN TRAD. EST.
DESERONTO TRADING EST.
RICHMOND CR.
KEITH CL.
APSLEY HO.
DIAMOND RD.
COLONIAL RD.
AUSTRALIA RD.
CANADA RD.
INDIA RD.
PRINCES ST.
VICTORIA RD.
EASTBRIDGE
St. Bernard's Prep. Sch.
Burial Gd.
GILMORE
KING'S CROFT
BRACKENFORDE
RAVENSFIELD
CHERRY
A4
Sub. Superstore
Sorting Off.
LOCKE GS.
DOLPHIN
OBSERVATORY
83
82
81
180
99
500

WOOLLEY GREEN
A404(M)
A404(M) MOTORWAY
6
Vanwall Business Park
Desborough Park
Factory
Works
Cox Green Sch.
Lowbrook Prim. Sch.
Playing Field
Sch.
The Old Cottage
Foundry
WOODLANDS PARK
THE MAIDENHEAD BUSINESS CAMPUS
COX GREEN
Lowbrook Farm
Lillibrooke Manor
Ockwells Home Farm
Ockwells Manor House
West London Aero Club
White Waltham Airfield
WOODLANDS BUSINESS PARK
Woodlands Park Prim. Sch.
Maidenhead
Great Thrift Wood
Little Thrift Wood
SL6
Heywood Cottages
Heywood Farm
Shrubbery Copse
Heywood Park Cottages
Filter Beds
Sewage Works
Waltham Grange
White Waltham
Wks.
Burycourt Farm
Waltham Place
M4 MOTORWAY
Paddock Wood
Brook Leys
Ormandy House
Kennels
New Cottages
BROADMOOR RD.
LITTLEFIELD GREEN
B3024
M4
Paley Street Farm
Beam End
Foxley Green Farm
Farmside
Longchase Farm
TOUCHEN END
Littlefield Green
Whitehouse Farm
PALEY STREET
Steppers
Short Lane Farm
Cedars House
Whites Farm
GREAT WOOD
PALEY ST.
The Cut
A B C D E
1 2 3 4 5 6 7
86 87 180 79 78 77

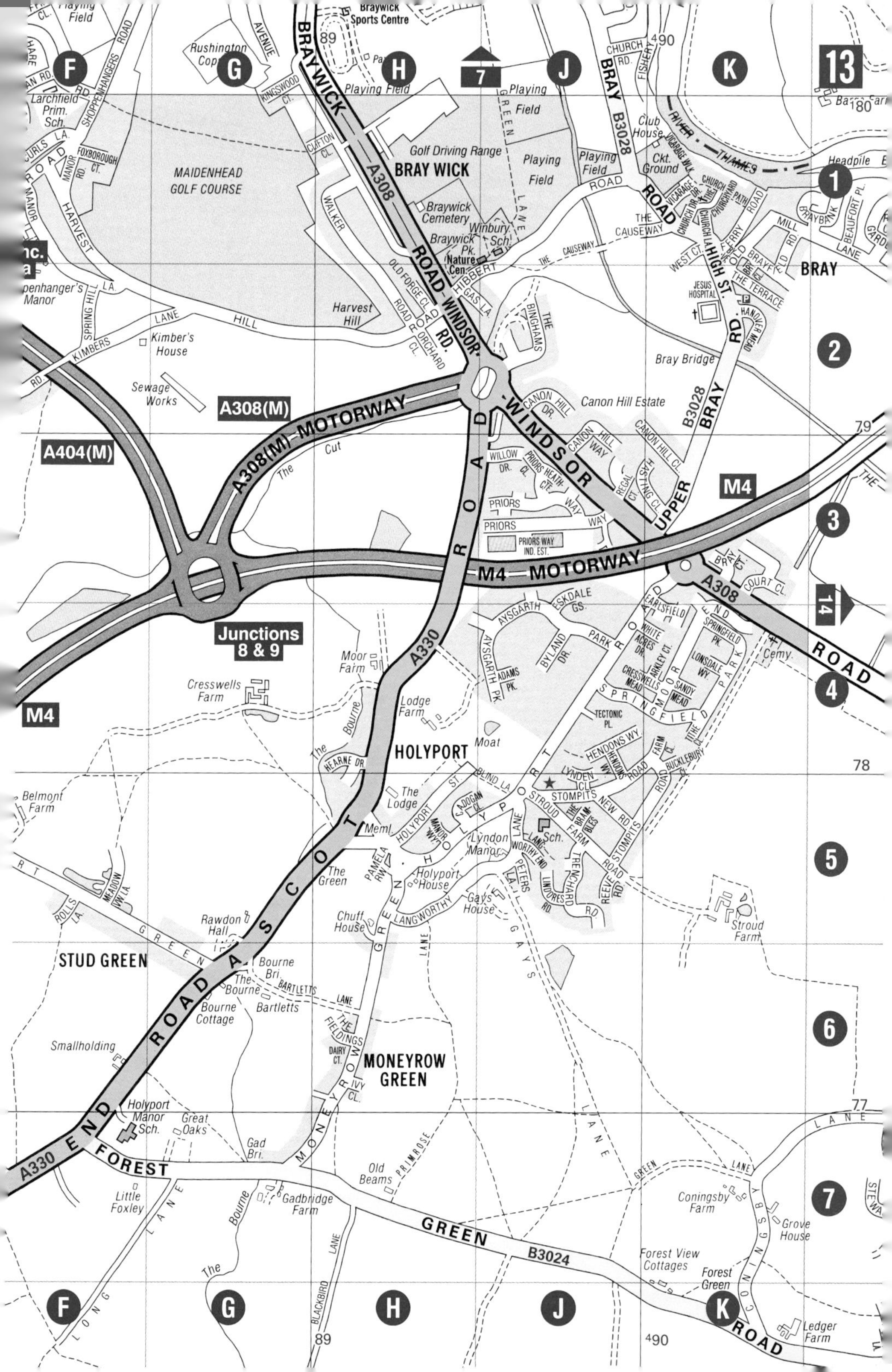

F
G
H
J
K
7
14
1
2
3
4
5
6
7
89
490
79
78
77
180
Braywick Sports Centre
Rushington Copse
Larchfield Prim. Sch.
SHOPPENHANGERS ROAD
KINGSWOOD CT.
CLIFTON CL.
BRAYWICK
Playing Field
Golf Driving Range
BRAY WICK
MAIDENHEAD GOLF COURSE
A308
WALKER
Braywick Cemetery
Braywick Pk.
Nature Cen.
Winbury Sch.
HIBBERT
GAS LA.
OLD FORGE CL.
ORCHARD CL.
ROAD
WINDSOR
Harvest Hill
HARVEST HILL
FOXBOROUGH CT.
SPRING HILL LA.
KIMBERS LANE
Kimber's House
Sewage Works
Shoppenhanger's Manor
A308(M)
A308(M) MOTORWAY
A404(M)
The Cut
M4 MOTORWAY
M4
Junctions 8 & 9
CHURCH RD.
FISHERY
BRAY
B3028
Club House
Ckt. Ground
RIVER THAMES
Headpile
VICARAGE WLK.
CHURCH DR.
CHURCH LA.
CHURCHYARD PATH
FERRY ROAD
MILL LANE
BRAYBANK
BEAUFORT PL.
THE CAUSEWAY
WEST CT.
HIGH ST.
OLD MILL LA.
BRAYFIELD RD.
THE TERRACE
JESUS HOSPITAL
HANOVER MEAD
THE BINGHAMS
Bray Bridge
CANON HILL DR.
CANON HILL WAY
Canon Hill Estate
CANON HILL CL.
UPPER BRAY RD.
REGAL CT.
HASTINGS CL.
WILLOW DR.
PRIORS HEATH CTE.
PRIORS WAY
PRIORS WAY IND. EST.
BRAY CT.
COURT CL.
A308 ROAD
AYSGARTH
ESKDALE GS.
AYSGARTH PK.
ADAMS PK.
BYLAND DR.
PARK ROAD
EARLSFIELD
WHITE ACRES DR.
ARKLEY CT.
CRESSWELLS MEAD
MOOR
SANDY MEAD
SPRINGFIELD PK.
LONSDALE WY.
SPRINGFIELD
END
PARK
THE CL.
Cemy.
TECTONIC PL.
HENDONS WY.
ROAD FARM CL.
BUCKLEBURY CL.
LYNDEN CL.
STOMPITS
NEW RD.
STOMPITS ROAD
Moor Farm
Cresswells Farm
A330
Lodge Farm
Moat
HOLYPORT
The Bourne
HEARNE DR.
BLIND LA.
HOLYPORT ST.
CADOGAN CL.
MANOR WY.
The Lodge
Meml.
Lyndon Manor
STROUD FARM
THE BRAMBLES
Sch.
WORTHY END
TRENCHARD RD.
REEVE RD.
LINDORES RD.
PETERS LA.
GAYS LANE
Gays House
Holyport House
PAMELA RW.
HOLYPORT GREEN
LANGWORTHY LANE
Chuff House
The Green
ASCOT ROAD
Belmont Farm
MEADOW VW. LA.
ROLLS LA.
GREEN
Rawdon Hall
STUD GREEN
Bourne Bri.
BARTLETTS LANE
Bartletts
The Bourne
Bourne Cottage
THE FIELDINGS
DAIRY CT.
IVY CL.
MONEYROW GREEN
Smallholding
Holyport Manor Sch.
Great Oaks
Gad Bri.
A330 END ROAD
FOREST
Old Beams
PRIMROSE LANE
Stroud Farm
LANE
Little Foxley
LONG LANE
The Bourne
Gadbridge Farm
GREEN B3024
BLACKBIRD LANE
Coningsby Farm
CONINGSBY LANE
Grove House
Forest View Cottages
Forest Green
ROAD
Ledger Farm

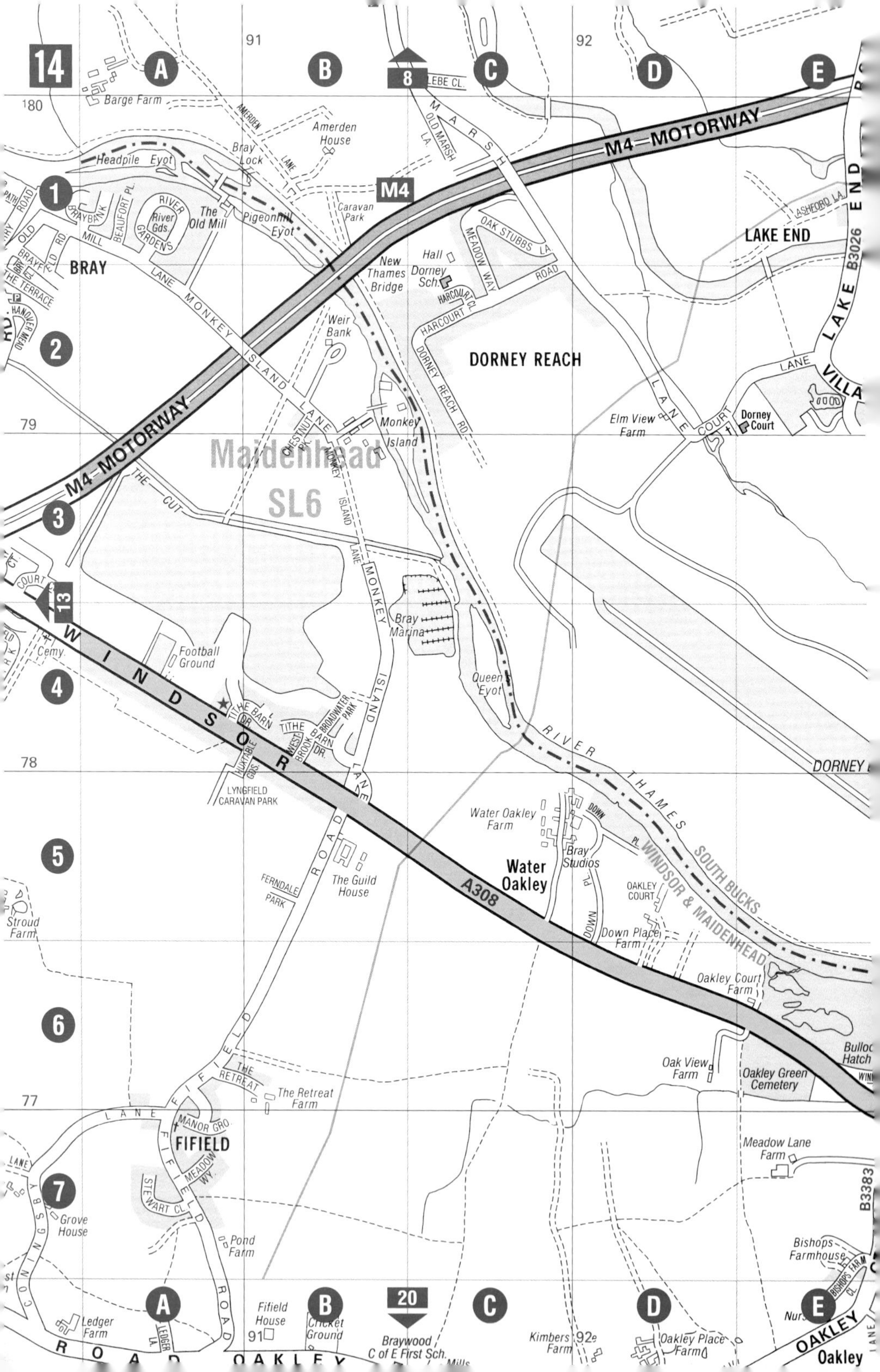

A
B
C
D
E
91
92
180
79
78
77
1
2
3
4
5
6
7
8
13
20
Barge Farm
Amerden House
AMERDEN LANE
Headpile Eyot
Bray Lock
The Old Mill
Pigeonhill Eyot
River Gds.
RIVER GARDENS
BEAUFORT PL.
BRAYBANK
MILL LANE
OLD MILL
BRAYFIELD RD.
THE TERRACE
HANOVER MEAD
BRAY
MONKEY ISLAND LANE
M4
M4–MOTORWAY
Caravan Park
LEBE CL.
MARSH
OLD MARSH LA.
New Thames Bridge
Weir Bank
Hall
Dorney Sch.
OAK STUBBS LA.
MEADOW WAY
HARCOURT CL.
HARCOURT ROAD
DORNEY REACH RD.
DORNEY REACH
LANE
ASHFORD LA.
LAKE END
B3026
LAKE END
VILLA
LANE
COURT
Dorney Court
Elm View Farm
Monkey Island
CHESTNUT PL.
Maidenhead
SL6
THE CUT
Bray Marina
Queen's Eyot
COURT
Cemy.
Football Ground
WINDSOR ROAD
TITHE BARN DR.
TITHE BARN DR.
WEST BROOK
BROADWATER PARK
HUXTABLE GDS.
LYNGFIELD CARAVAN PARK
RIVER THAMES
DORNEY
Water Oakley Farm
DOWN PL.
Bray Studios
Water Oakley
The Guild House
FERNDALE PARK
ROAD
A308
WINDSOR & MAIDENHEAD
SOUTH BUCKS
OAKLEY COURT
Down Place Farm
Oakley Court Farm
Stroud Farm
Bullock Hatch
Oak View Farm
Oakley Green Cemetery
THE RETREAT
The Retreat Farm
FIFIELD
LANE
MANOR GRO.
FIFIELD
MEADOW WY.
STEWART CL.
Meadow Lane Farm
B3383
Grove House
Pond Farm
CONINGSBY
Bishops Farmhouse
BISHOPS FARM CL.
Ledger Farm
LEDGER LA.
ROAD
OAKLEY
Fifield House
Cricket Ground
Braywood C of E First Sch.
Kimbers Farm
Oakley Place Farm
OAKLEY
Oakley

15
Junction 7
M4-MOTORWAY
M4
Slough
SL1
Mercian Way Rec. Grd.
Sludge Beds
Filter Beds
Water Pollution Control Works
Pipe Line Station
Superstore
JUBILEE RIVER
Weir
Roundmoor Ditch
ETON LITTLE COMMON
Long Close
Eton Common Farm
Woodpeckers
SLOUGH SOUTH BUCKS
SLOUGH WINDSOR & MAIDENHEAD
ETON WICK
Manor Fm.
Court Farm
Riding School
Tilson Bri.
Saddocks Farm
Manor Farm
Bell Farm
DORNEY COMMON
COMMON ROAD
ETON WICK ROAD
B3026
ETON GREAT COMMON
Crown Farm
Elm Farm Bungalow
Eton Wick Rec. Grd.
Boveney Ditch
Windsor
SL4
Cress Brook
Stamford
ROASTHILL LANE
BOVENEY ROAD
Boveney Court Farm
Boveney
LOCK PATH
Boveney Court
Boveney Lock
THAMES
RIVER
Water Jump
Athens
MEADOW LANE
ROYAL WINDSOR RACECOURSE
Parade Ring
Grand Stand
Upper Hope
Cuckoo Weir
Windsor Racecourse Yacht Basin
Toll
Dorney Lake Rowing Centre
Mill Stream
Clewer St. Andrew
Works
Ruddles Pool
MAIDENHEAD ROAD
A308
CLEWER VILLAGE
Cemy.
Youth Cen.
Comm. Cen.
Play. Field
Rec. Grd.
Fitness Club
DEDWORTH
Playing Field
Schools
Lib.
B3025 ROAD
VALE
B3024
DEDWORTH ROAD
CLARENCE RD.
IMPERIAL RD.
PARSONAGE
BROOM FARM ESTATE
9
16
21
79
78
77
94
495

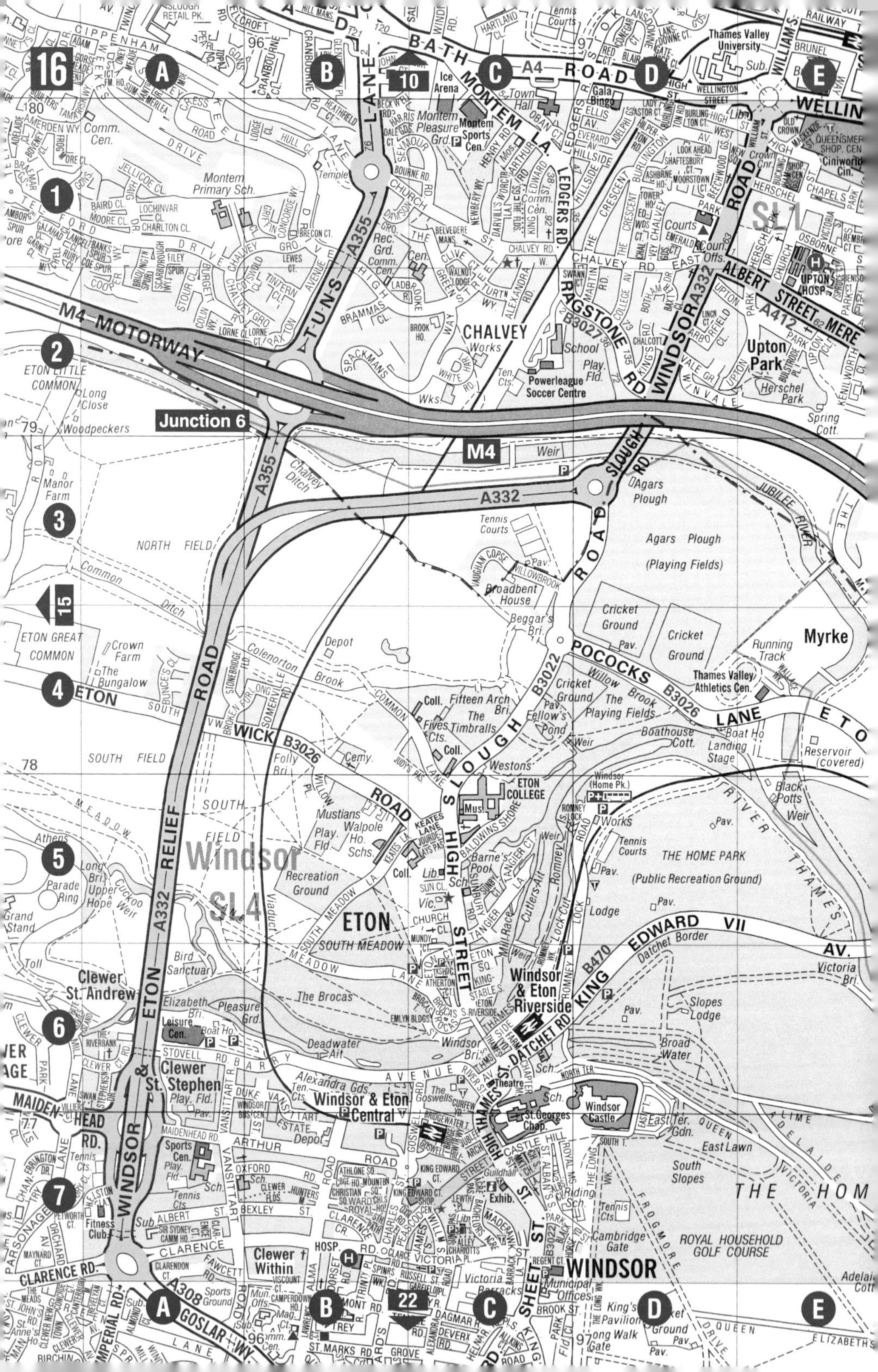

BATH ROAD
A4
Thames Valley University
WELLINGTON STREET
Ice Arena
Montem Sports Cen.
Montem Pleasure Grd.
Town Hall
MONTEM LA.
LEDGERS RD
Montem Primary Sch.
TUNS LANE
A355
CHALVEY
CHALVEY RD.
RAGSTONE RD.
WINDSOR RD.
A332
ALBERT STREET
A412
Upton Park
Herschel Park
SL1
Powerleague Soccer Centre
M4 MOTORWAY
M4
Junction 6
ETON LITTLE COMMON
Long Close
Woodpeckers
Manor Farm
NORTH FIELD
Common Ditch
ETON GREAT COMMON
Crown Farm
The Bungalow
Agars Plough
Agars Plough (Playing Fields)
Broadbent House
Beggar's Bri.
Cricket Ground
POCOCKS LANE
B3026
Myrke
Running Track
Thames Valley Athletics Cen.
ETON WICK ROAD
SOUTH FIELD
Colenorton Brook
Fifteen Arch Bri.
The Timbralls
SLOUGH ROAD
B3022
The Playing Fields
Willow Brook
Boathouse Cott.
Boat Ho Landing Stage
Reservoir (covered)
Black Potts Weir
RIVER THAMES
ETON COLLEGE
HIGH STREET
Mustians Play. Fld.
Walpole Ho. Schs.
Recreation Ground
Windsor SL4
ETON
SOUTH MEADOW
Viaduct
THE HOME PARK
(Public Recreation Ground)
KING EDWARD VII AV.
Datchet Border
Victoria Bri.
Romney Lock
Lock Cut
Cutlers Ait
Windsor & Eton Riverside
Windsor (Home Pk.)
The Brocas
Deadwater Ait
Windsor Bri.
ETON RELIEF ROAD
A332
Athens
Long Bri.
Upper Hope
Parade Ring
Cuckoo Weir
Grand Stand
Bird Sanctuary
Clewer St. Andrew
Elizabeth Bri.
Pleasure Grd.
Leisure Cen.
Clewer St. Stephen
Alexandra Gds.
Windsor & Eton Central
Windsor Castle
St. Georges Chap.
East Ter. Gdn.
Slopes Lodge
Broad Water
East Lawn
South Slopes
THE HOME PARK
ROYAL HOUSEHOLD GOLF COURSE
Cambridge Gate
FROGMORE
Guildhall
Theatre
DATCHET RD
B470
THAMES ST.
MAIDENHEAD RD.
Sports Cen.
Fitness Club
CLARENCE RD.
Clewer Within
Victoria Barracks
Municipal Offices
WINDSOR
King's Pavilion
Long Walk Gate
QUEEN ELIZABETH
A308
GOSLAR WY.
Sports Ground
22
10
15

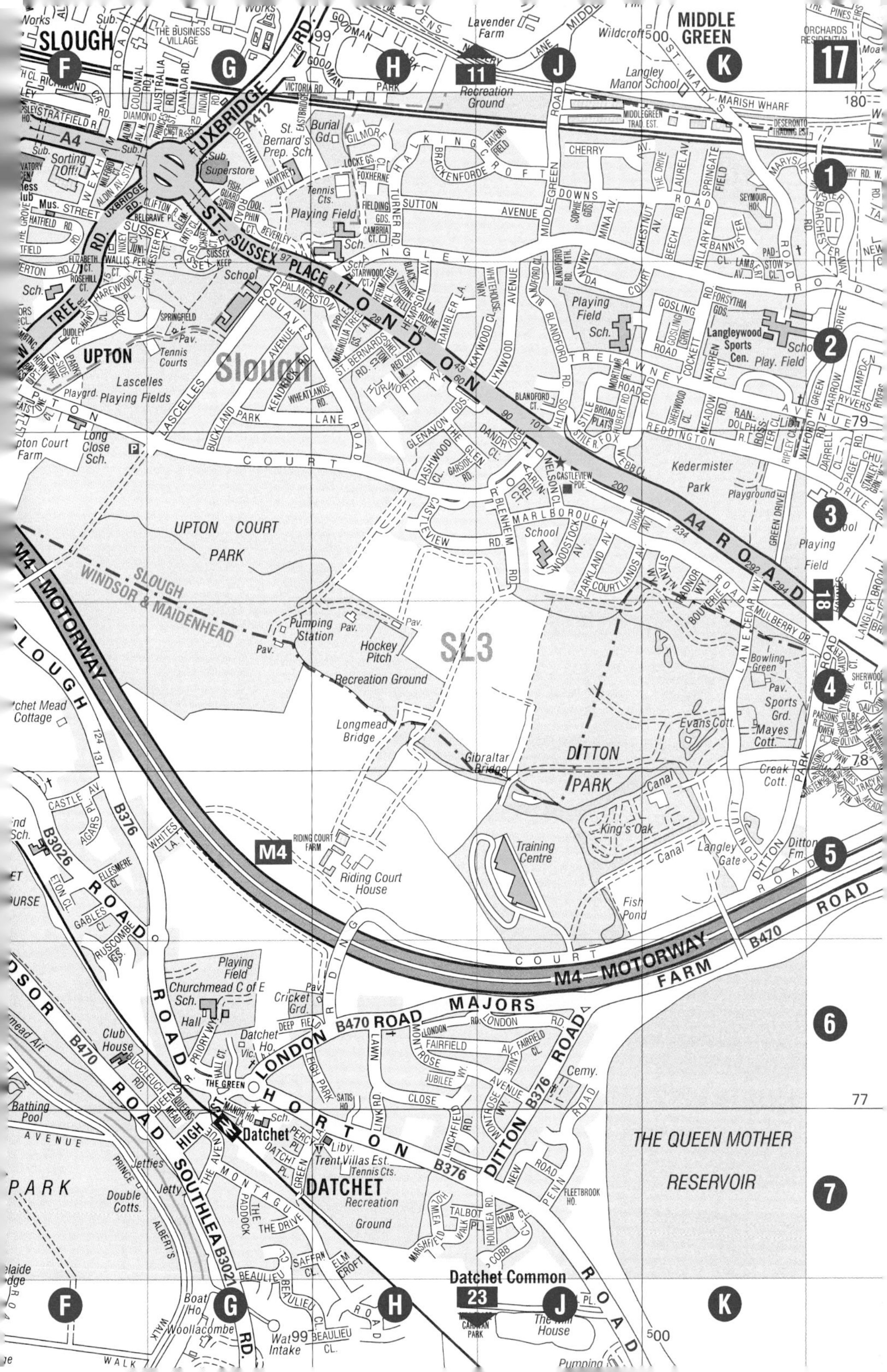

17
SLOUGH
MIDDLE GREEN
Lavender Farm
Wildcroft
Langley Manor School
Recreation Ground
THE BUSINESS VILLAGE
UXBRIDGE RD.
A412
A4
St. Bernard's Prep. Sch.
Burial Gd.
Superstore
Sorting Off.
Mus.
UPTON
Lascelles Playing Fields
Tennis Courts
Slough
LONDON ROAD
SUSSEX PLACE
ST. LAURENCE WAY
LANGLEY ROAD
Playing Field
Sch.
Langleywood Sports Cen.
Play. Field
Kedermister Park
Playground
A4 ROAD
CASTLEVIEW PDE.
School
Upton Court Farm
Long Close Sch.
UPTON COURT PARK
SLOUGH
WINDSOR & MAIDENHEAD
M4 MOTORWAY
Pumping Station
Hockey Pitch
Recreation Ground
SL3
Longmead Bridge
Gibraltar Bridge
DITTON PARK
Canal
King's Oak
Training Centre
Riding Court House
RIDING COURT FARM
M4
Bowling Green
Sports Grd.
Evans Cott.
Mayes Cott.
Creak Cott.
Ditton Fm.
Langley Gate
Fish Pond
Datchet Mead Cottage
B376
B3026
B470
Playing Field
Churchmead C of E Sch.
Hall
Club House
Cricket Grd.
Datchet Ho.
THE GREEN
Datchet
DATCHET
Liby.
Trent Villas Est.
Tennis Cts.
Recreation Ground
Cemy.
HORTON ROAD
MAJORS FARM ROAD
THE QUEEN MOTHER RESERVOIR
Bathing Pool
PARK
Jetties
Double Cotts.
SOUTHLEA ROAD
B3021
Boat Ho.
Woollacombe
Wat Intake
Datchet Common
23
The Mill House
18
11
F G H J K
1 2 3 4 5 6 7

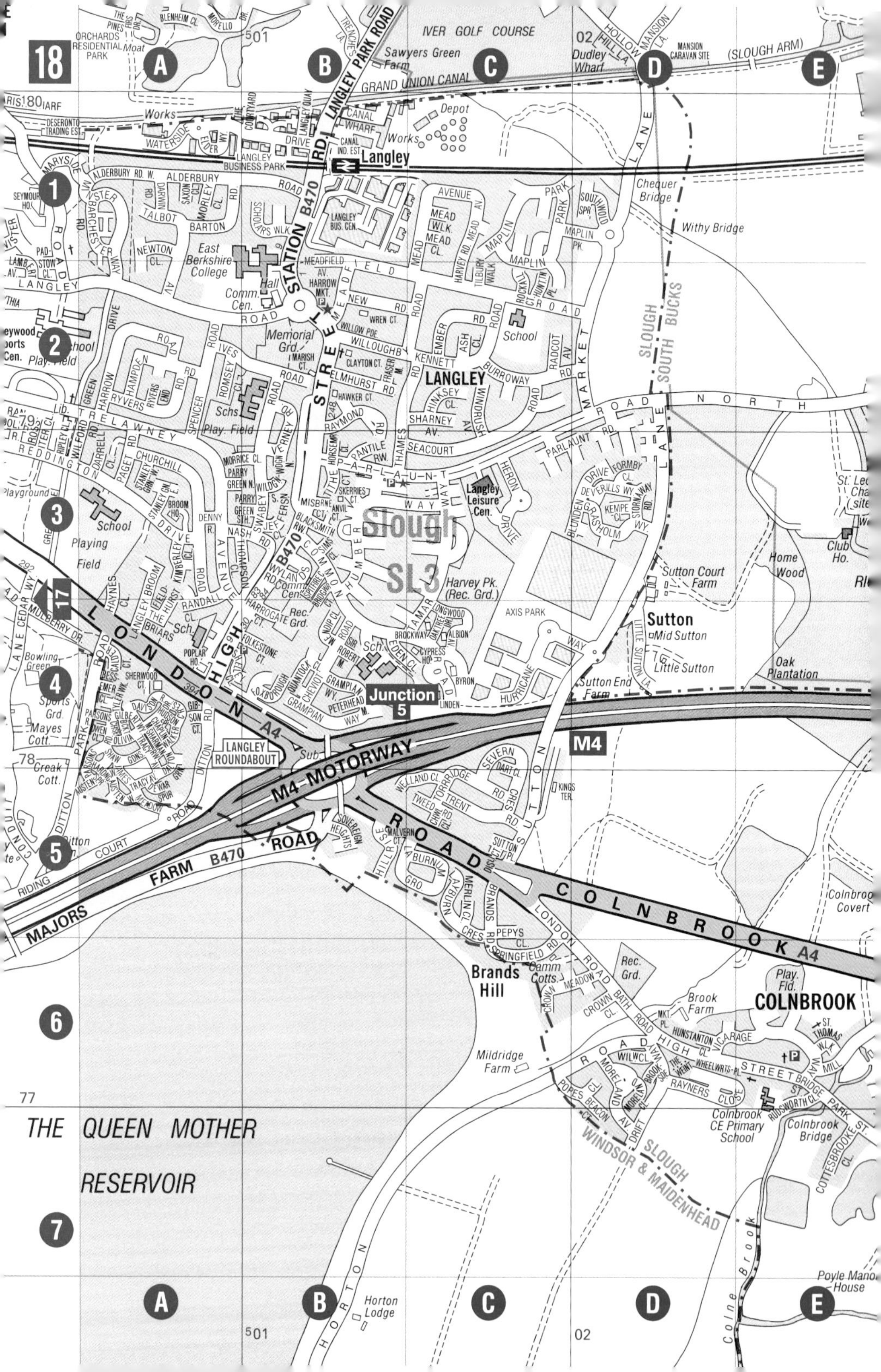

IVER GOLF COURSE
Sawyers Green Farm
GRAND UNION CANAL
Dudley Wharf
MANSION CARAVAN SITE
(SLOUGH ARM)
ORCHARDS RESIDENTIAL PARK
Moat
Works
Depot
LANGLEY BUSINESS PARK
Langley
LANGLEY PARK ROAD
STATION RD. B470
Chequer Bridge
Withy Bridge
East Berkshire College
Comm. Cen.
Memorial Grd.
LANGLEY
School
SLOUGH
SOUTH BUCKS
Schs.
Play. Field
Playground
Playing Field
Slough SL3
Langley Leisure Cen.
Harvey Pk. (Rec. Grd.)
AXIS PARK
Sutton Court Farm
Sutton
Mid Sutton
Little Sutton
Home Wood
Club Ho.
Oak Plantation
Sutton End Farm
Junction 5
M4
M4 MOTORWAY
LANGLEY ROUNDABOUT
LONDON ROAD A4
MAJORS FARM B470 ROAD
RIDING COURT
Bowling Green
Sports Grd.
Mayes Cott.
Creak Cott.
COLNBROOK A4
Brands Hill
Rec. Grd.
Mildridge Farm
Brook Farm
Play. Fld.
COLNBROOK
Colnbrook CE Primary School
Colnbrook Bridge
Colnbrook Covert
WINDSOR & MAIDENHEAD
SLOUGH
THE QUEEN MOTHER RESERVOIR
Horton Lodge
Poyle Manor House
Colne Brook
A B C D E
1 2 3 4 5 6 7
501
02
77
78
79
80

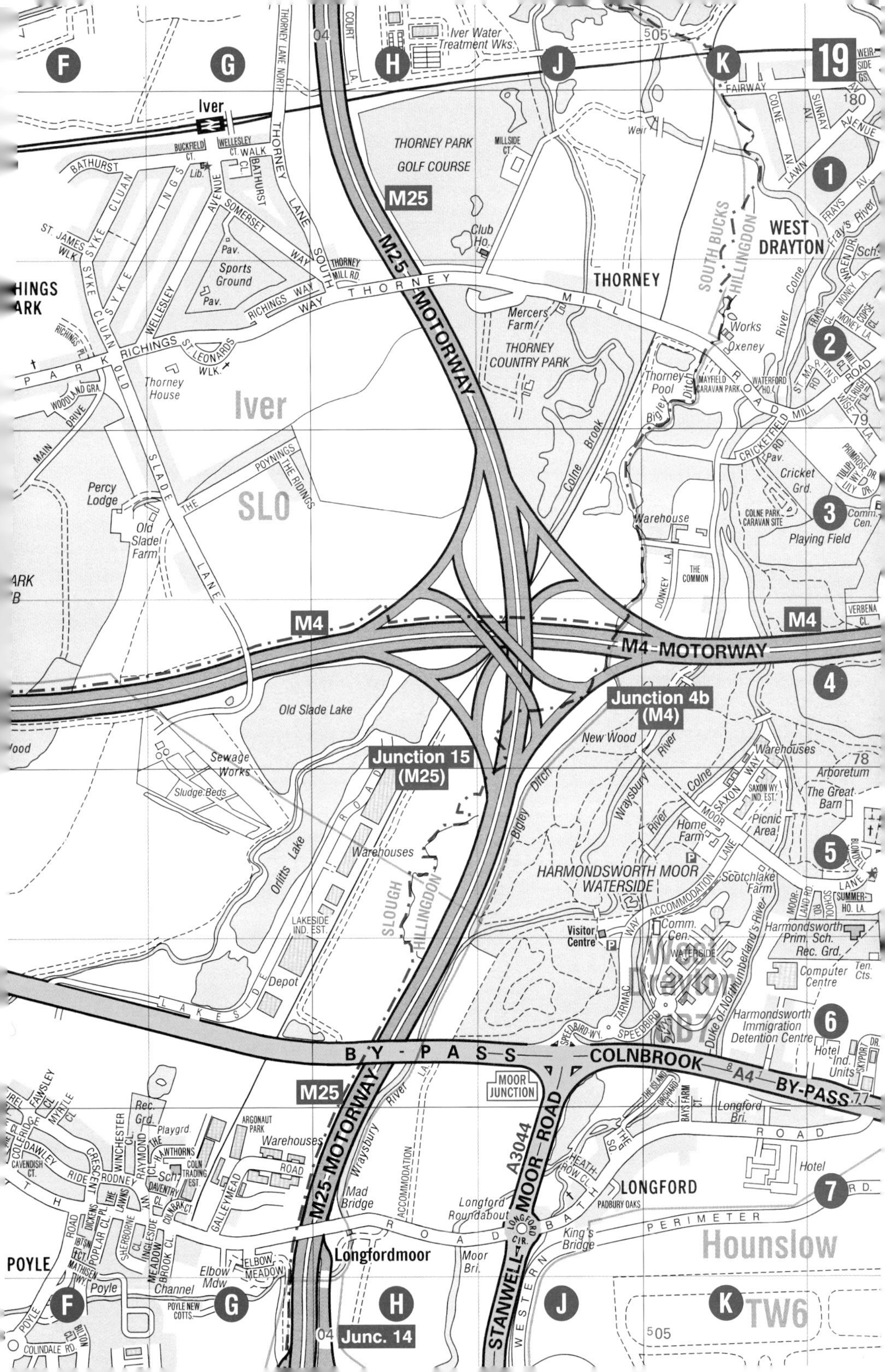
F
G
H
J
K
F
G
H
J
K
1
2
3
4
5
6
7
04
505
04
505
80
79
78
77
Iver
Iver Water
Treatment Wks.
THORNEY LANE NORTH
COURT LA.
FAIRWAY
COLNE AV.
SUNRAY AV.
AVENUE
WEIR SIDE GS
LAWN AV.
FRAYS AV.
Fray's River
WEST DRAYTON
BUCKFIELD CT.
WELLESLEY CT.
WALK CL.
Lib.
BATHURST
CLUAN
SYKE
INGS
AVENUE
SOMERSET
THORNEY
LANE
SOUTH
WAY
ST. JAMES WLK.
THORNEY PARK
GOLF COURSE
MILLSIDE CT.
M25
Club Ho.
Weir
SOUTH BUCKS
HILLINGDON
Pav.
Sports Ground
Pav.
THORNEY MILL RD.
RICHINGS WAY
WAY THORNEY
MILL
THORNEY
HINGS
ARK
RICHINGS PL.
PARK
OLD
RICHINGS
ST. LEONARDS WLK.
Thorney House
WOODLAND GRA.
DRIVE
MAIN
Iver
M25 MOTORWAY
Mercers Farm
THORNEY COUNTRY PARK
Works
Oxeney
Thorney Pool
Bigley Ditch
MAYFIELD CARAVAN PARK
ROAD
MILL
WATERFORD HO.
ST. MARTINS RD.
ROAD
Colne
River
Sch.
WREN DR.
MONEY LA.
MONEY LA.
COPSE CL.
FRAYS CL.
MILL CL.
WISE LA.
LA.
CRICKETFIELD RD.
Pav.
Cricket Grd.
PRIMROSE DR.
TULIP WY.
LILY DR.
COLNE PARK CARAVAN SITE
Comm. Cen.
Playing Field
Percy Lodge
Old Slade Farm
SLADE
LANE
THE POYNINGS
THE RIDINGS
SLO
Colne Brook
Warehouse
DONKEY LA.
THE COMMON
ARK
B
M4
M4
VERBENA CL.
M4 MOTORWAY
Junction 4b
(M4)
Wood
Old Slade Lake
New Wood
River
Warehouses
Arboretum
The Great Barn
Sewage Works
Sludge Beds
Junction 15
(M25)
ROAD
Bigley Ditch
Wraysbury
Colne
SAXON WAY
SAXON WY. IND. EST.
MOOR LANE
River
Home Farm
Picnic Area
BLONDELL LANE
Orlitts Lake
Warehouses
SLOUGH
HILLINGDON
HARMONDSWORTH MOOR
WATERSIDE
ACCOMMODATION
WAY
Scotchlake Farm
MOOR LANE RD.
SCHOOL RD.
SUMMERHO. LA.
LAKESIDE IND. EST.
Visitor Centre
Comm. Cen.
WATERSIDE
West Drayton
UB7
Duke of Northumberland's River
Harmondsworth Prim. Sch.
Rec. Grd.
Ten. Cts.
Depot
LAKESIDE
TARMAC
SPEEDBIRD
SPEEDBIRD WY.
Computer Centre
Harmondsworth Immigration Detention Centre
Hotel
Ind. Units
SKYPORT DR.
BY-PASS
COLNBROOK
A4
BY-PASS
MOOR JUNCTION
M25
FAWSLEY CL.
MYRTLE CL.
COLERIDGE CL.
DAWLEY
CAVENDISH CT.
RIDE
CRESCENT
WINCHESTER CL.
Rec. Grd.
RAYMOND CL.
Playgrd.
THE HAWTHORNS
Sch.
DAVENTRY CL.
COLN TRADING EST.
COLNBROOK CT.
RODNEY
THE LAWNS
ARGONAUT PARK
Warehouses
ROAD
GALLEYMEAD
M25 MOTORWAY
Wraysbury
River
LA.
Mad Bridge
ACCOMMODATION
A3044
MOOR
ROAD
THE ISLAND
ORCHARD PL.
BAYS FARM CT.
Longford Bri.
ROAD
THE
HEATHROW CL.
Hotel
LONGFORD
PADBURY OAKS
BATH
Longford Roundabout
LONGFORD CIR.
King's Bridge
PERIMETER
RD.
Hounslow
ROAD
DICKENS PL.
POPLAR CL.
SHERBORNE CL.
INGLESIDE
MEADOW
BROOK CL.
IBTSN
ICT.
MATHISEN WY.
POYLE
Poyle
Channel
Elbow Mdw
ELBOW MEADOW
POYLE NEW COTTS.
Longfordmoor
Moor Bri.
WESTERN
STANWELL
TW6
Junc. 14
COLINDALE RD.
BILTON CL.
POYLE

20
14
A
B
C
D
E
1
2
3
4
5
6
7
91
92
76
175
74
73
Maidenhead
SL6
Grove House
Pond Farm
WART CL.
FIFIELD ROAD
CONINGSBY LA.
Ledger Farm
LEDGER LA.
FOREST GREEN ROAD
B3024
Banham Farm
Fifield House
Cricket Ground
Braywood C of E First Sch.
Mills Farm
OAKLEY GREEN
Kimbers Lane Farm
Kimbers Farm
BRAYWOOD COTTS.
Oakley Place Farm
Forest Farm
Bishops Farm House
BISHOPS FARM CL.
Nursery
Oakley Green
Gale House Farm
TARBAY LA.
Tarbay Farm
FIFIELD LANE
Braywood House
Grave Yard
Bray Wood
Darkhole Bri.
DARKHOLE RIDE
HOLLIDAY'S PLAIN
Nightingale Corner
DRIFT
New Lodge Farm
New Lodge
Queen Charlotte's Tree
Nobbscrook
Garden Cottage
Greenways
The Bolt
Nobbscrook Cottages
Nobbscrook Farm
Queen Anne's Tree
FORBE'S RIDE
Nobbscrook Copse
Windsor Hill
Fish Pond
Lawn Hill
FOLIEJON PARK
Home Farm
Home Covert
DRIFT ROAD
Bray Paddock
Forbe's Fields
Pumproom Copse
Orchard Lea
The Pump Room
Winkfield Place
Winkfield Plain Farm
The Godown
Barton Lodge Farm
Bad Br
BADGERSBRIDGE
SCHOOL
WINKFIELD LANE
Old Dairy Farm
Listowel
LAKE VIEW CARAVAN SITE
Tally Ho Farm
CROUCH LANE
Smoothfield Farm Kennels
Ash Farm
Burton Lodge
Tennis Court
Five Acres
Hope Farm
Tow's Bourne
Florence Cottages
MILLSIDE PARK
Great Oaks Farm
Greatoaks Cott.
CRANBOURNE
Cranbourne Hall
CRANBOURNE HALL CARAVAN SITE
CRANBOURNE HALL COTTS.
SPINNEY LA.
THE PADDOCK
BROADWAY
THE COPSE
BERKELEY DR.
SQUIRRELL LA.
THORNE WY.
WELLINGTON LODGE
Ranelagh Farm
Poplars Farm
Offices
B3022
NORTH STREET
Radio and Space Research Station
Nursery

21
DEDWORTH
Dedworth Green
Clewer Green
Clewer New Town
Clewer Hill
Windsor
SL4
B3024
B3022
B3175
A332
B383
CLARENCE RD.
IMPERIAL
ST. LEONARD'S RD.
THAMES VALLEY HOSPICE
Windsor Girls' Sch.
CEMETERY
Windsor & Eton FC (Stag Meadow)
St. Leonardshill
Reservoirs (covered)
Water Tower
St. Leonard's Farm
St. Leonard's
LEGOLAND
Windsor (Legoland)
Government Lodge
Lodge
Crown Cotts.
Withy Cover
Ash Plantation
Diningroom Close
Spital Meadow
Paddockhill Copse
Palatine Gate
New Cover
CONSORT'S DRIVE
Flemish Farm
Bromley Hill
Star Clump
PRINCE CONSORT'S DRIVE
Queen Victoria's Tree
High Standinghill Woods
BRACKNELL FOREST
WINDSOR & MAIDENHEAD
High Standing Hill
Fish Pond
Forest Park
Park Pale
CRANBOURNE WOOD
CRANBOURNE CHASE
Devil's Gap
Cranbourne Covert
Buck Paddocks
Brook's Corner
Pickleherring Pond
CRANBOURNE PARK
Reservoir (covered)
Cranbourne Tower
SHEET STREET ROAD
Ranger's Gate
Ranger's Lodge
Beehive Plantation
Beehive Hill
Fiddle Covert
Russel's Pond
Russel's Plantation
WINKFIELD
PLAIN RIDE
TOWER RIDE
QUELMANS HEAD RIDE
DSOR FOREST
15
22
F G H J K
1 2 3 4 5 6 7
94
495
175
74
73

WINDSOR
NEW WINDSOR
Clewer New Town
Clewer Within
ROYAL HOUSEHOLD GOLF COURSE
Frogmore
Frogmore House
Royal Mausoleum
Mausoleum
Frogmore Cott.
Frogmore Lake
Jubilee Mount
Tea Room
Victoria Barracks
Municipal Offs.
King's Pavilion
Long Walk Gate
Cricket Ground
Cambridge Gate
GOSLAR WAY
A308
OSBORNE RD.
FRANCES RD.
ALMA RD
B3175 ROAD
IMPERIAL
ST. LEONARD'S
B3022
KING'S ROAD
A332
SHEET STREET
ALBERT
Princess Margaret Hosp.
Household Cavalry Museum
Spital
CEMETERY
Windsor & Eton FC (Stag Meadow)
Bourne Ditch
Moat
Queen Mary's Plantation
Park Pale
Miniature Rifle Range
Spital Meadow
Cavalry Exercise Grounds
CONSORT'S DRIVE
PRINCE
Review Ground
HOG COMMON
Garrison Sports Ground
Queen Annes Gate Cott.
Arklow Cott.
Shaw Farm
Crown Cottages
North Lodge
Shawfarm Gate
Albert Lodge
Windsor
Clayhall Farm
South Lodge
SL4
Tileplace Farm
Petershill Copse
Newmeadow Plantation
Crimp Hill Cemetery
Bear's Rails
Bear's Rails Gate
Rush Pond
Bear's Rails Pond
Scout Camp
Old Windsor Wood
Star Clump
Flemish Farm
Sir Andrew Cope's Clump
Ranger's Gate
Beehive Plantation
Beehive Hill
Prince of Wales Pond
Sandy Arch
Battle Bourne
THE GALLOP
QUEEN ANNE'S RIDE
THE LONG WALK
Seymours Plantation
Withy Bed
Liddell Plantation
Fiddle Covert
Russel's Pond
Russel's Plantation
Marchioness of Hertford Plantation
Duke of York Plantation
Prince Consort's Plantation
Sultan Plantation
Old Covert
A B C D E
1 2 3 4 5 6 7
96 97 175 74 73 76
16 21

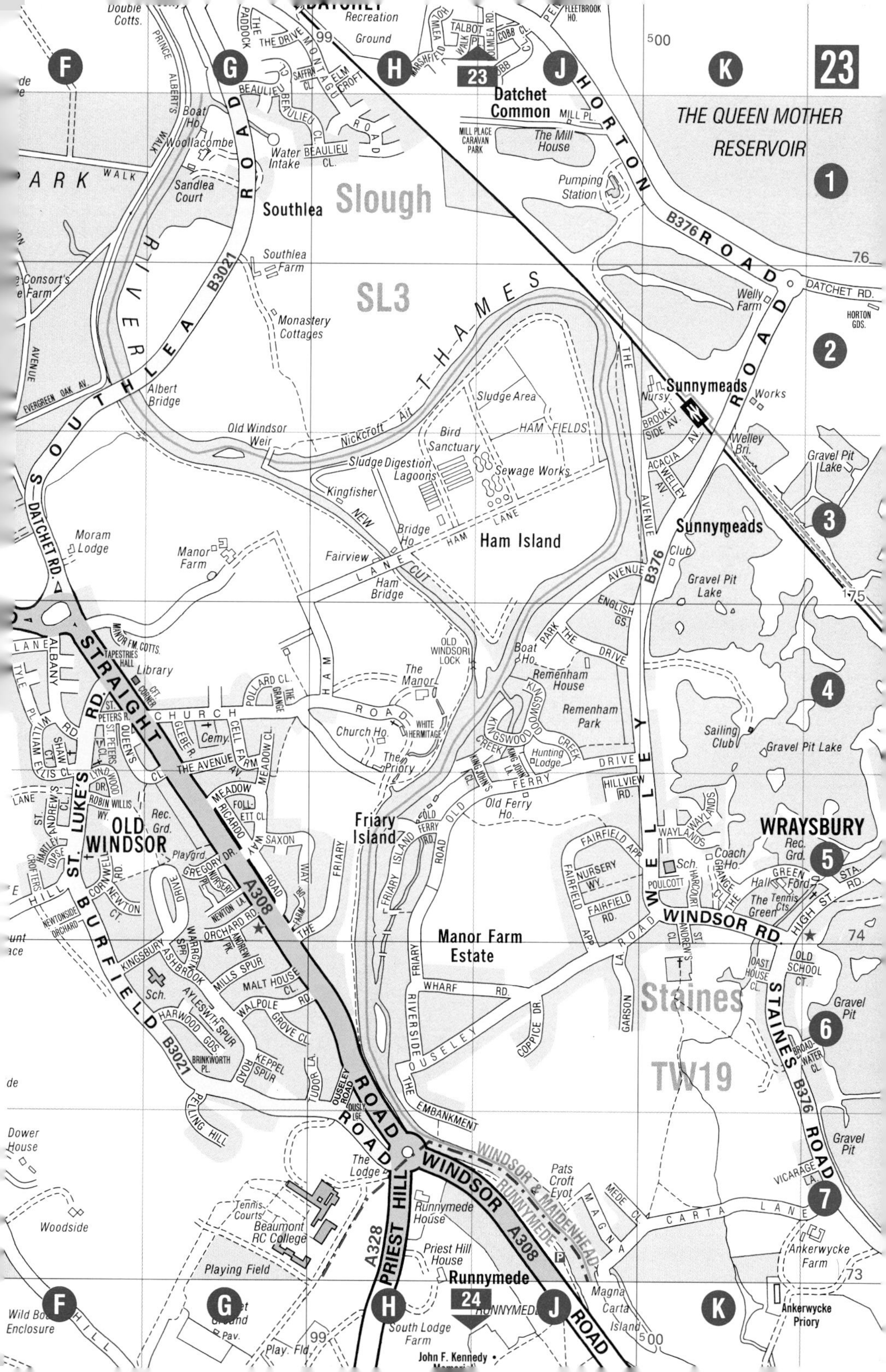
F
G
H
J
K
23
DATCHET
Recreation
Ground
Double
Cotts.
THE PADDOCK
THE DRIVE
MONTAGU
BEAULIEU CL.
SAFFRON CL.
ELM CROFT
MARSHFIELD
TALBOT
WALK PL.
HOLMLEA
OLMLEA RD.
COBB CL.
FLEETBROOK HO.
500
Datchet
Common
MILL PL.
MILL PLACE CARAVAN PARK
The Mill House
HORTON
THE QUEEN MOTHER
RESERVOIR
1
PRINCE ALBERT'S WALK
Boat Ho.
Woollacombe
Water Intake
BEAULIEU CL.
PARK WALK
Sandlea Court
Southlea
Slough
Pumping Station
B376 ROAD
RIVER
Southlea Farm
76
SL3
THAMES
Consort's Farm
Monastery Cottages
B3021
SOUTHLEA ROAD
Welly Farm
DATCHET RD.
HORTON GDS.
2
AVENUE
EVERGREEN OAK AV.
Albert Bridge
Sludge Area
THE AVENUE
Sunnymeads
Nursy.
BROOKSIDE AV.
Works
Old Windsor Weir
Nickcroft Ait
Bird Sanctuary
HAM FIELDS
ACACIA AV.
WELLEY AV.
Welley Bri.
Gravel Pit Lake
Sludge Digestion Lagoons
Sewage Works
Kingfisher
NEW CUT
3
Moram Lodge
Bridge Ho.
HAM LANE
Ham Island
Sunnymeads
DATCHET RD.
Manor Farm
Fairview
B376
Club
Gravel Pit Lake
Ham Bridge
AVENUE
175
ENGLISH GS.
MANOR FM. COTTS.
LANE
ALBANY
TAPESTRIES HALL
Library
STRAIGHT
OLD WINDSOR LOCK
Boat Ho.
PARK
THE DRIVE
Remenham House
4
TYLE PL.
CT. CORNER
POLLARD CL.
THE GRANGE
HAM ROAD
The Manor
Remenham Park
RD.
ST. PETERS RD.
CHURCH
WHITE HERMITAGE
KINGSWOOD
KINGSWOOD CREEK
Sailing Club
WILLIAM ELLIS CL.
SHAW CT.
ST. PETERS CL.
GLEBE RD.
Cemy.
CELL FARM AV.
Church Ho.
Hunting Lodge
Gravel Pit Lake
LYNDWOOD DR.
QUEEN'S CL.
THE AVENUE
MEADOW CL.
The Priory
KING JOHN'S CL.
KING JOHN LA.
DRIVE
LANE
ROBIN WILLIS WY.
MEADOW WAY
FERRY
HILLVIEW RD.
ST. ANDREW'S CL.
ST. LUKE'S RD.
OLD WINDSOR
Rec. Grd.
FOLLIETT CL.
RICARDO
Friary Island
Old Ferry Ho.
OLD FERRY DR.
WAYLANDS
WRAYSBURY
HARTLEY COPSE
CROFTERS
Playgrd.
GREGORY DR.
SAXON WAY
FRIARY ISLAND
WELLEY
Rec. Grd.
HILL
CORNWELL RD.
NEWTON CT.
NURSERY
FARM
FRIARY ROAD
FAIRFIELD APP.
Sch.
Coach Ho.
5
BURFIELD
NEWTONSIDE ORCHARD
DRIVE
NEWTON LA.
ORCHARD RD.
A308
NURSERY WY.
POULCOTT
HARCOURT
GRANGE
GREEN
Hall
Ford
STA. RD.
WARRINGTON SPR
ANDREW PK.
THE
FAIRFIELD RD.
ST. ANDREW'S CL.
WINDSOR RD.
The Green
Tennis Cts.
HIGH ST.
KINGSBURY
ASHBROOK
Manor Farm
Estate
LA. ROAD
74
MILLS SPUR
OLD SCHOOL CT.
Sch.
MALT HOUSE CL.
WHARF RD.
OAST HOUSE CL.
AYLESWORTH SPUR
WALPOLE RD.
Staines
Gravel Pit
HARWOOD GDS.
GROVE CL.
RIVERSIDE
COPPICE DR.
GARSON LA.
6
BRINKWORTH PL.
KEPPEL SPUR
STAINES
BROADWATER CL.
B3021
OUSELEY
TW19
B376
PELLING HILL
TUDOR LA.
OUSELEY ROAD
THE EMBANKMENT
Gravel Pit
Dower House
OUSLY. LGE.
ROAD
ROAD
WINDSOR & MAIDENHEAD
RUNNYMEDE
Pats Croft Eyot
VICARAGE LA.
The Lodge
MEDE CL.
7
Tennis Courts
Woodside
Beaumont RC College
Runnymede House
MAGNA
CARTA LANE
A328
PRIEST HILL
WINDSOR
A308
Priest Hill House
Ankerwycke Farm
Playing Field
Runnymede
73
Magna Carta Island
Wild Boar Enclosure
HILL
24
RUNNYMEDE
Pav.
South Lodge Farm
99
Play. Fld.
500
Ankerwycke Priory
John F. Kennedy

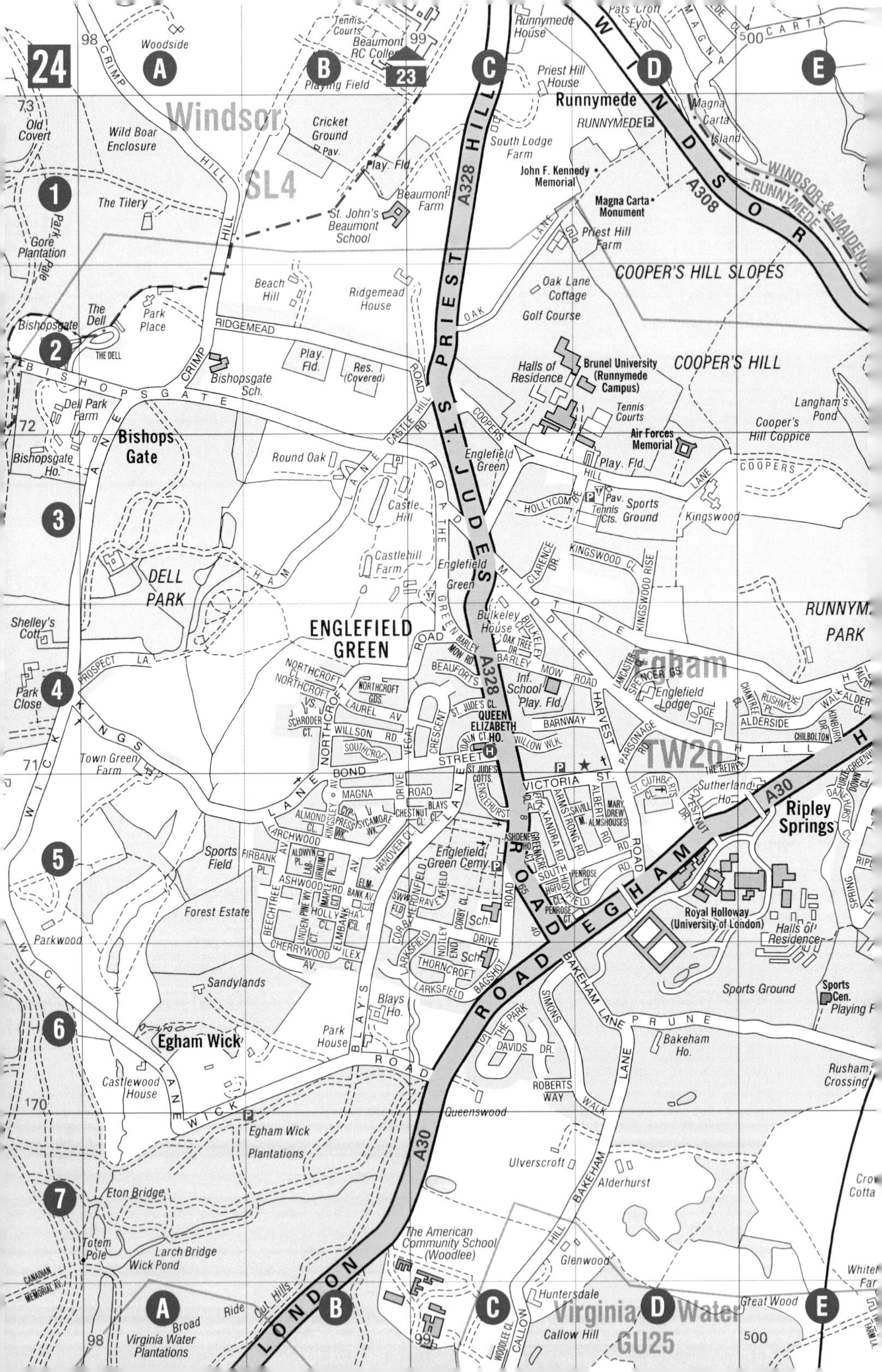
23
A
B
C
D
E
1
2
3
4
5
6
7
Woodside
Tennis Courts
Beaumont RC College
Playing Field
Runnymede House
Pats Croft Eyot
Priest Hill House
Runnymede
RUNNYMEDE
Windsor
SL4
Old Covert
Wild Boar Enclosure
Cricket Ground
Pav.
Play. Fld.
South Lodge Farm
John F. Kennedy Memorial
Magna Carta Island
Magna Carta Monument
WINDSOR-&-MAIDENHEAD
RUNNYMEDE
A308
WINDSOR
CARTA
MAGNA
The Tilery
Beaumont Farm
St. John's Beaumont School
A328
PRIEST HILL
Priest Hill Farm
Gore Plantation
Park Pale
CRIMP HILL
COOPER'S HILL SLOPES
Beach Hill
Ridgemead House
Oak Lane Cottage
Golf Course
The Dell
Bishopsgate
THE DELL
Park Place
RIDGEMEAD
OAK LANE
Play. Fld.
Res. (Covered)
Halls of Residence
Brunel University (Runnymede Campus)
COOPER'S HILL
Bishopsgate Sch.
BISHOPSGATE
Dell Park Farm
Bishops Gate
Tennis Courts
Air Forces Memorial
Langham's Pond
Cooper's Hill Coppice
Bishopsgate Ho.
Round Oak
CASTLE HILL RD.
COOPERS
Englefield Green
Play. Fld.
COOPERS HILL LANE
HOLLYCOMBE
Pav.
Tennis Cts.
Sports Ground
Kingswood
Castle Hill
DELL PARK
HAM LANE
Castlehill Farm
Englefield Green
CLARENCE DR.
KINGSWOOD CL.
KINGSWOOD RISE
MIDDLE HILL
Shelley's Cott.
ENGLEFIELD GREEN
Bulkeley House
BULKELEY CL.
OAK TREE DR.
BARLEY MOW RD.
RUNNYMEDE PARK
Egham
Park Close
PROSPECT LA.
NORTHCROFT CL.
NORTHCROFT VS.
NORTHCROFT GDS.
BEAUFORTS
Inf. School
Play. Fld.
LANCASTER CL.
SPENCER GS.
Englefield Lodge
CHANTREE CL.
RUSHMERE PL.
ALDERSIDE
ALDER CL.
KINBURN DR.
CHILBOLTON
LAUREL AV.
SCHRODER CT.
WILLSON RD.
ST. JUDE'S CL.
QUEEN ELIZABETH HO.
BARNWAY
HARVEST RD.
PARSONAGE RD.
TW20
HILL
THE RETREAT
KINGS LANE
SOUTHCROFT
CRESCENT
TORIN CT.
WILLOW WLK.
Town Green Farm
BOND STREET
ST. JUDE'S COTTS.
VICTORIA ST.
ST. CUTHBERTS CL.
Sutherland Ho.
A30
Ripley Springs
FURZE DOWN
DANEHURST CL.
MAGNA ROAD
ENGLEHURST
ARMSTRONG RD.
ALBERT RD.
MARY DREW ALMSHOUSES
SAVILL M.
CHESTNUT DR.
ALMOND CL.
CYPRESS WK.
SYCAMORE WK.
CHESTNUT CL.
BLAYS CL.
HANOVER CL.
ASHDENE HO.
ALEXANDRA RD.
LARCHWOOD
ALDWYN PL.
LABURNUM
Sports Field
FIRBANK PL.
Englefield Green Cemy.
GREENACRE CT.
SOUTH
HIGHFIELD
PENROSE CT.
EGHAM HILL
Royal Holloway (University of London)
Halls of Residence
SPRING
ASHWOOD RD.
MAPLE CT.
ELMBANK AV.
Forest Estate
BEECHTREE AV.
PINE WY.
LINDEN CT.
HOLLY CL.
ELMBANK
HA CL.
SWW FLD
HERONFIELD
RAVENFIELD
CORBY CL.
Sch.
Parkwood
CHERRYWOOD AV.
ILEX CL.
NOTLEY END
DRIVE
Sch.
THORNCROFT
LARKSFIELD
BAGSHOT ROAD
BAKEHAM LANE
Sports Ground
Sports Cen.
Sandylands
Blays Ho.
SIMONS WALK
WICK LANE
WICK ROAD
Egham Wick
Park House
BLAY'S LANE
THE PARK
ST. DAVIDS DR.
PRUNE HILL
Bakeham Ho.
Rusham Crossing
Castlewood House
ROBERTS WAY
Queenswood
Egham Wick Plantations
Ulverscroft
BAKEHAM LANE
Alderhurst
Eton Bridge
Totem Pole
Larch Bridge
Wick Pond
The American Community School (Woodlee)
Glenwood
CANADIAN MEMORIAL AV.
Huntersdale
LONDON ROAD
Ride
Broad
Out Hills
Virginia Water Plantations
Virginia Water
GU25
Callow Hill
CALLOW HILL
WOODLEE CL.
Great Wood
98
99
500
73
72
71
170
65
40

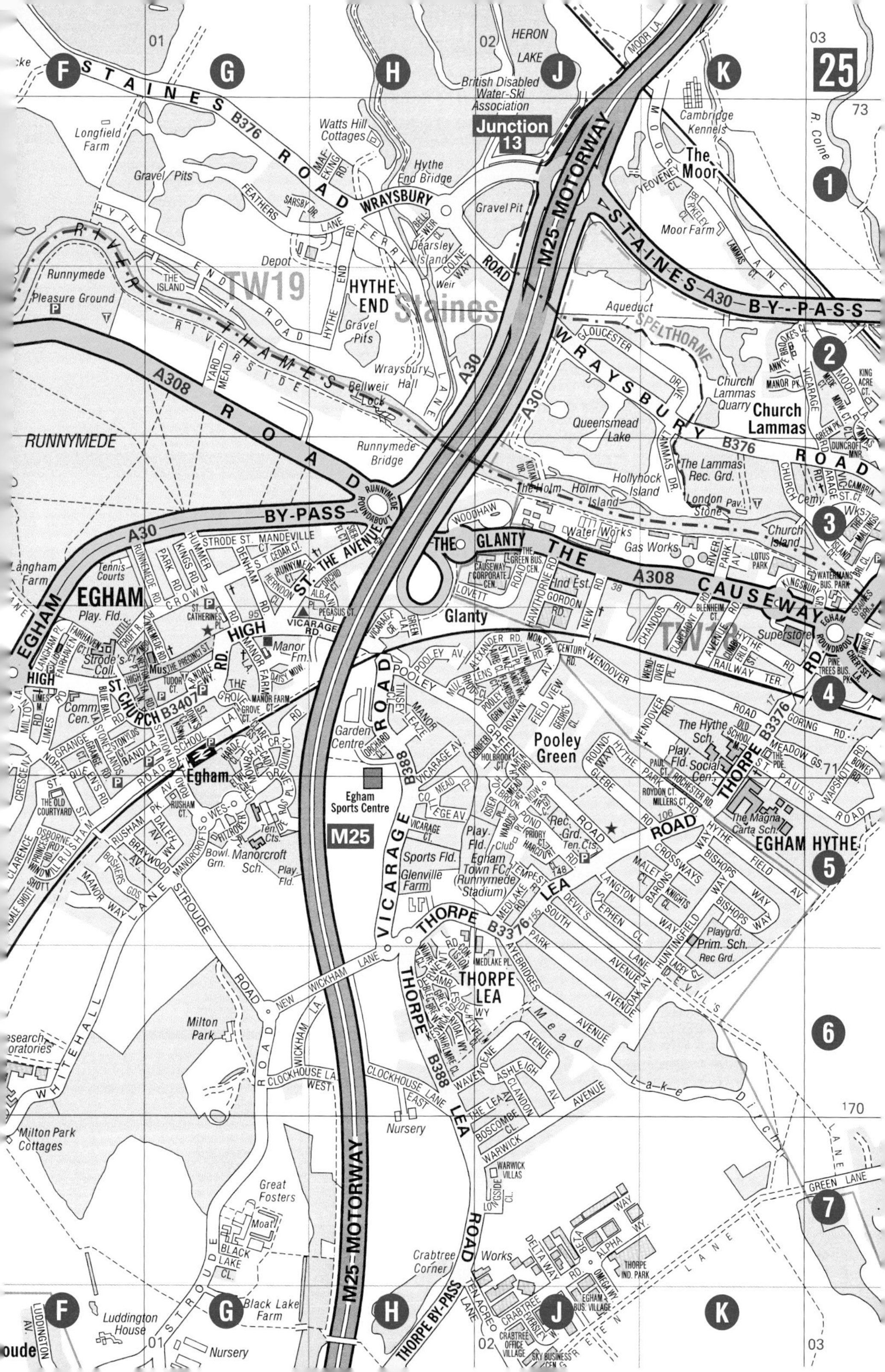

F
G
H
J
K
1
2
3
4
5
6
7
01
02
03
73
71
170
STAINES ROAD B376
Longfield Farm
Gravel Pits
HERON LAKE
British Disabled Water-Ski Association
Junction 13
Watts Hill Cottages
Hythe End Bridge
WRAYSBURY ROAD
Gravel Pit
M25 MOTORWAY
Cambridge Kennels
The Moor
Moor Farm
R. Colne
STAINES A30 BY-PASS
Aqueduct
SPELTHORNE
RIVER THAMES
Runnymede Pleasure Ground
Depot
Dearsley Island
TW19
HYTHE END
Staines
Gravel Pits
Wraysbury Hall
Bellweir Lock
A308 ROAD
WRAYSBURY ROAD
Church Lammas Quarry
Church Lammas
Queensmead Lake
B376 ROAD
RUNNYMEDE
Runnymede Bridge
RUNNYMEDE ROUNDABOUT
The Holm
Holm Island
Hollyhock Island
The Lammas Rec. Grd.
London Stone
Church Island
A30 BY-PASS
THE GLANTY
Water Works
Gas Works
Langham Farm
Tennis Courts
EGHAM
THE CAUSEWAY A308
Glanty
Ind Est.
TW18
Superstore
EGHAM ROUNDABOUT
Play. Fld.
EGHAM HIGH
HIGH ST.
Strode's Coll.
Mus.
Manor Fm.
Comm. Cen.
CHURCH RD. B3407
Egham
POOLEY AV.
POOLEY GREEN RD.
Pooley Green
Garden Centre
Egham Sports Centre
M25
The Hythe Sch.
Play. Fld.
Social Cen.
THORPE RD. B3376
The Magna Carta Sch.
EGHAM HYTHE
Manorcroft Sch.
Bowl. Grn.
Play. Fld.
Sports Fld.
Glenville Farm
Play. Fld.
Egham Town FC (Runnymede Stadium)
Rec. Grd.
Ten. Cts.
THORPE LEA ROAD B3376
Playgrd.
Prim. Sch.
Rec Grd.
THORPE LEA
VICARAGE ROAD B388
NEW WICKHAM LANE
STROUDE ROAD
Milton Park
Research Laboratories
WHITEHALL LANE
CLOCKHOUSE LANE
THORPE B388
Mead AVENUE
Lake Di tch
Nursery
Milton Park Cottages
Great Fosters
Moat
BLACK LAKE CL.
LEA ROAD
WARWICK VILLAS
GREEN LANE
Crabtree Corner
Works
THORPE IND. PARK
EGHAM BUS. VILLAGE
CRABTREE OFFICE VILLAGE
SKY BUSINESS CEN.
THORPE BY-PASS
Black Lake Farm
Luddington House
Nursery
LUDDINGTON AV.

INDEX

Including Streets, Places & Areas, Hospitals & Hospices, Industrial Estates, Selected Flats & Walkways, Junction Names, Stations and Selected Places of Interest.

HOW TO USE THIS INDEX

1. Each street name is followed by its Postcode District and then by its Locality abbreviation(s) and then by its map reference; e.g. **Abbey Pk. La.** SL1: Burn . . . .1A **4** is in the SL1 Postcode District and the Burnham Locality and is to be found in square 1A on page **4**. The page number is shown in bold type.

2. A strict alphabetical order is followed in which Av., Rd., St., etc. (though abbreviated) are read in full and as part of the street name; e.g. **Ash Cl.** appears after **Ashbrook Rd.** but before **Ashcroft Ct.**

3. Streets and a selection of flats and walkways too small to be shown on the maps, appear in the index with the thoroughfare to which it is connected shown in brackets; e.g. **Alexandra Ct.** *SL4: Wind . . . .1C **22** (off Alexandra Rd.)*

4. Addresses that are in more than one part are referred to as not continuous.

5. Places and areas are shown in the index in **BLUE TYPE** and the map reference is to the actual map square in which the town centre or area is located and not to the place name shown on the map; e.g. **BISHOPS GATE 2A 24**

6. An example of a selected place of interest is **Berkshire Yeomanry Mus. 3C 22**

7. An example of a station is **Burnham Station (Rail) 5G 9**

8. Junction names are shown in the index in **BOLD CAPITAL TYPE**; e.g. **LANGLEY RDBT. 5B 18**

9. An example of a hospital or hospice is **HRH PRINCESS CHRISTIAN'S HOSPITAL 7B 16**

GENERAL ABBREVIATIONS

All. : Alley
App. : Approach
Av. : Avenue
Bri. : Bridge
Bldgs. : Buildings
Bus. : Business
Cvn. : Caravan
Cen. : Centre
Cir. : Circus
Cl. : Close
Coll. : College
Comn. : Common
Cnr. : Corner
Cott. : Cottage
Cotts. : Cottages
Ct. : Court
Cres. : Crescent
Cft. : Croft
Dr. : Drive
E. : East
Ent. : Enterprise
Est. : Estate
Fld. : Field
Flds. : Fields
Gdns. : Gardens
Ga. : Gate
Gt. : Great
Grn. : Green
Gro. : Grove
Hgts. : Heights
Ho. : House
Ind. : Industrial
Info. : Information
Junc. : Junction
La. : Lane
Lit. : Little
Lwr. : Lower
Mnr. : Manor
Mans. : Mansions
Mkt. : Market
Mdw. : Meadow
Mdws. : Meadows
M. : Mews
Mt. : Mount
Mus. : Museum
Nth. : North
Pde. : Parade
Pk. : Park
Pas. : Passage
Pl. : Place
Res. : Residential
Ri. : Rise
Rd. : Road
Rdbt. : Roundabout
Shop. : Shopping
Sth. : South
Sq. : Square
Sta. : Station
St. : Street
Ter. : Terrace
Trad. : Trading
Up. : Upper
Va. : Vale
Vw. : View
Vs. : Villas
Vis. : Visitors
Wlk. : Walk
W. : West
Yd. : Yard

LOCALITY ABBREVIATIONS

Bray : **Bray**
Burn : **Burnham**
Coln : **Colnbrook**
Dat : **Datchet**
Dor : **Dorney**
Dor R : **Dorney Reach**
Egh : **Egham**
Eng G : **Englefield Green**
Eton : **Eton**
Eton W : **Eton Wick**
Farn C : **Farnham Common**
Farn R : **Farnham Royal**
Fifi : **Fifield**
Ful : **Fulmer**
G Grn : **George Green**
Ger X : **Gerrards Cross**
Harm : **Harmondsworth**
Hedg : **Hedgerley**
Holy : **Holyport**
Hort : **Horton**
Iver : **Iver**
L'ly : **Langley**
Lit G : **Littlewick Green**
H'row A : **London Heathrow Airport**
Lford : **Longford**
Maid : **Maidenhead**
Oak G : **Oakley Green**
Old Win : **Old Windsor**
Pal S : **Paley Street**
Poyle : **Poyle**
Rich P : **Richings Park**
Slou : **Slough**
Staines : **Staines**
Stoke P : **Stoke Poges**
Tap : **Taplow**
Thorn : **Thorney**
Thorpe : **Thorpe**
Vir W : **Virginia Water**
Wat O : **Water Oakley**
W Dray : **West Drayton**
Wex : **Wexham**
W Walt : **White Waltham**
Wind : **Windsor**
Wink : **Winkfield**
Wray : **Wraysbury**

A

Abbey Cl. SL1: Slou 6H **9**
Abbey Pk. La. SL1: Burn 1A **4**
Abbots Wlk. SL4: Wind 1H **21**
Abbotts Way SL1: Slou 7G **9**
Abell Gdns. SL6: Maid 3C **6**
Aberdeen Av. SL1: Slou 6K **9**
Abingdon Wlk. SL6: Maid 1F **7**
Acacia Av. TW19: Wray 3K **23**
Accommodation La. UB7: Harm 5K **19**
UB7: Lford 7H **19**
Acre Pas. SL4: Wind 7C **16**
Adam Cl. SL1: Slou 7K **9**
Addington Cl. SL4: Wind 2K **21**
Addison Ct. SL6: Maid 3J **7**
Adelaide Cl. SL1: Slou 1K **15**
Adelaide Rd. SL4: Wind 7E **16**
Adelaide Sq. SL4: Wind 1C **22**
Adelphi Gdns. SL1: Slou 1D **16**
Adrians Wlk. SL2: Slou 7E **10**
Agars Pl. SL3: Dat 5F **17**
Aintree Cl. SL3: Poyle 7F **19**
Air Forces Memorial 3D **24**
Ajax Av. SL1: Slou 6A **10**
Alan Way SL3: G Grn 5K **11**
Albany Pk. SL3: Coln 7E **18**
Albany Pl. TW20: Egh 3H **25**
Albany Rd. SL4: Old Win 4F **23**
SL4: Wind 1C **22**
Albert Cl. SL1: Slou 2E **16**
Albert Pl. SL4: Eton W 4K **15**
Albert Rd. SL4: Old Win, Wind 2C **22**
TW20: Eng G 5D **24**
Albert St. SL1: Slou 2E **16**
(not continuous)
SL4: Wind 7A **16**
SL6: Maid 6G **7**
(not continuous)
Albion SL3: L'ly 4C **18**
Albion Cl. SL2: Slou 7F **11**
Albion Pl. SL4: Wind 1K **21**
Aldborough Spur SL1: Slou 5D **10**
Aldbourne Rd. SL1: Burn 4E **8**
Aldebury Rd. SL6: Maid 2F **7**
Alden Vw. SL4: Wind 7G **15**
Alderbury Rd. SL3: L'ly 1A **18**
Alderbury Rd. W. SL3: L'ly 1A **18**
Alder Cl. SL1: Slou 7J **9**
TW20: Eng G 4E **24**
Alderside Wlk.
TW20: Eng G 4E **24**
Aldin Av. Nth. SL1: Slou 1F **17**
Aldin Av. Sth. SL1: Slou 1F **17**
Aldridge Rd. SL2: Slou 3K **9**
Aldwick Dr. SL6: Maid 6E **6**
Aldwyn Pl. TW20: Eng G 5B **24**
Alexander Rd. TW20: Egh 4J **25**
(not continuous)

Alexandra Ct. *SL4: Wind* *1C 22*
(off Alexandra Rd.)
Alexandra Rd. SL1: Slou 2C 16
SL4: Wind 1C 22
SL6: Maid 4E 6
TW20: Eng G 5C 24
Alice La. SL1: Burn 3E 8
Allenby Rd. SL6: Maid 5C 6
Allerds Rd. SL2: Farn R 7B 4
Allington Ct. SL2: Slou 5E 10
Allkins Ct. SL4: Wind 1C 22
All Saints Av. SL6: Maid 4D 6
Alma Ct. SL1: Burn 2F 9
Alma Rd. SL4: Eton W 3J 15
SL4: Wind 1B 22
Almond Cl. SL4: Wind 1A 22
TW20: Eng G 5B 24
Almond Rd. SL1: Burn 2F 9
Almons Way SL2: Slou 4G 11
Alpha St. Nth. SL1: Slou 1F 17
Alpha St. Sth. SL1: Slou 2E 16
Alpha Way TW20: Thorpe 7J 25
Alpine Cl. SL6: Maid 6H 7
Alston Gdns. SL6: Maid 5F 7
Altona Way SL1: Slou 5A 10
Altwood Bailey SL6: Maid 7C 6
Altwood Cl. SL1: Slou 4H 9
SL6: Maid 7C 6
Altwood Dr. SL6: Maid 7C 6
Altwood Rd. SL6: Maid 7B 6
(not continuous)
Alvista Av. SL6: Tap 5E 8
Alwyn Rd. SL6: Maid 4C 6
Alyson Ct. SL6: Maid 3G 7
Amanda Ct. SL3: L'ly 2J 17
Amberley Ct. SL6: Maid 1K 7
Amberley Pl. SL4: Wind 7C 16
Amberley Rd. SL2: Slou 4H 9
Ambleside Way TW20: Egh 6H 25
Amerden Cl. SL6: Tap 5A 8
Amerden La. SL6: Tap 5A 8
(Amerden Cl.)
SL6: Tap 1B 14
(River Gdns.)
Amerden Way SL1: Slou 1K 15
Andermans SL4: Wind 7G 15
Andrew Hill La. SL2: Hedg 1E 4
Ankerwycke Priory 1E 24
Anne Cl. SL6: Maid 2F 7
Annie Brookes Cl. TW18: Staines 2K 25
Ansculf Rd. SL2: Slou 2K 9
Anslow Pl. SL1: Slou 4F 9
Anthony Way SL1: Slou 6G 9
Anvil Ct. SL3: L'ly 3B 18
Apple Cft. SL6: Maid 2D 12
Appletree La. SL3: L'ly 2H 17
Approach Rd. SL6: Tap 5B 8
Apsley Ho. SL1: Slou 1F 17
Arborfield Cl. SL1: Slou 2D 16
Archer Cl. SL6: Maid 4E 6
Arches, The *SL4: Wind* *7B 16*
(off Goswell Rd.)
Ardrossan Cl. SL2: Slou 3B 10
Argent Cl. TW20: Egh 5J 25
Argonaut Pk. SL3: Poyle 7G 19
Argyll Av. SL1: Slou 6K 9
Arkley Ct. SL6: Holy 4K 13
Arlington Cl. SL6: Maid 4A 6
Armstrong Rd. TW20: Eng G 5C 24
Arndale Way TW20: Egh 4G 25
Arthur Rd. SL1: Slou 1C 16
SL4: Wind 7B 16
Arundel Cl. SL6: Maid 4B 6
Arundel Ct. SL3: L'ly 3J 17
Ascot Rd. SL6: Holy 6G 13
Ashbourne Gro. SL6: Maid 2D 12
Ashbourne Ho. SL1: Slou 1D 16
Ashbrook Rd. SL4: Old Win 6G 23
Ash Cl. SL3: L'ly 2C 18
Ashcroft Ct. SL1: Burn 1E 8
Ashcroft Rd. SL6: Maid 4D 6
Ashdene Ho. TW20: Eng G 5C 24
Ashdown SL6: Maid 1J 7
Ashenden Wlk. SL2: Farn C 3F 5
Ashford La. SL4: Dor 1E 14
Ash Gro. SL2: Stoke P 6H 5
Ash La. SL4: Wind 1G 21
Ashleigh Av. TW20: Egh 6J 25
Ashley Ct. SL6: Maid 5J 7
Ashley Pk. SL6: Maid 2J 7
Ashton Pl. SL6: Maid 6B 6
Ashwood Rd. TW20: Eng G 5B 24
Aspen Cl. SL2: Slou 4A 10
Aston Mead SL4: Wind 7H 15
Astor Cl. SL6: Maid 6J 7
Atherton Ct. SL4: Eton 6C 16
Athlone Cl. SL6: Maid 3F 7
Athlone Sq. SL4: Wind 7B 16
Atkinson's All. SL6: Maid 4G 7
Auckland Cl. SL6: Maid 4J 7
Audley Dr. SL6: Maid 6C 6
August End SL3: G Grn 5K 11
Austen Vw. SL3: L'ly 5A 18
Austen Way SL3: L'ly 5A 18
Australia Av. SL6: Maid 4G 7
Australia Rd. SL1: Slou 1G 17
Autumn Cl. SL1: Slou 7J 9
Autumn Wlk. SL6: Maid 7B 6
Avebury SL1: Slou 6K 9
Avenue, The SL2: Farn C 3D 4
SL3: Dat 7G 17
SL4: Old Win 4G 23
SL6: Maid 2J 7
TW19: Wray 2J 23
TW20: Egh 3H 25
Avenue Rd. SL6: Maid 7J 7
TW18: Staines 4K 25
Averil Ct. SL6: Tap 5F 9
Avon Cl. SL1: Slou 6H 9
Avondale SL6: Maid 3D 6
Axis Pk. SL3: L'ly 4C 18
Ayebridges Av. TW20: Egh 6J 25
Aylesbury Cres. SL1: Slou 5C 10
Aylesworth Av. SL2: Slou 2A 10
Aylesworth Spur SL4: Old Win 6G 23
Aysgarth Pk. SL6: Holy 4J 13
Azalea Way SL3: G Grn 5K 11

B

Bachelors Acre SL4: Wind 7C 16
Bader Gdns. SL1: Slou 1K 15
Badger Cl. SL6: Maid 1E 12
Badgersbridge Ride SL4: Wink 6E 20
Badgers Wood SL2: Farn C 4E 4
Bad Godesberg Way SL6: Maid 5G 7
Badminton Rd. SL6: Maid 6C 6
Bagshot Rd. TW20: Eng G 6C 24
Bailey Cl. SL4: Wind 1K 21
SL6: Maid 5G 7
Baird Cl. SL1: Slou 1A 16
Bakeham La. TW20: Eng G 6D 24
Bakers La. SL6: Maid 4A 6
Bakers Row SL6: Maid 4A 6
Baldwin Pl. SL6: Maid 5D 6
Baldwin Rd. SL1: Burn 2F 9
Baldwins Shore SL4: Eton 5C 16
Ballard Grn. SL4: Wind 6H 15
Balmoral SL6: Maid 3C 6
Balmoral Cl. SL1: Slou 5H 9
Balmoral Gdns. SL4: Wind 2C 22
Banbury Av. SL1: Slou 4J 9
Band La. TW20: Egh 4F 25
Banks Spur SL1: Slou 1A 16
Bannard Rd. SL6: Maid 7B 6
Bannister Cl. SL3: L'ly 1K 17
Barchester Rd. SL3: L'ly 1A 18
Bardney Cl. SL6: Maid 2E 12
Bargeman Rd. SL6: Maid 1F 13
Barley Mead SL6: Maid 7B 6
Barley Mow Rd. TW20: Eng G 4C 24
Barn Cl. SL2: Farn C 3D 4
SL6: Maid 2G 7
Barn Dr. SL6: Maid 1B 12
Barnfield SL1: Slou 7G 9
Barnway TW20: Eng G 4C 24
Barons Way TW20: Egh 5K 25
Barrack La. SL4: Wind 7C 16
Barrow Lodge SL2: Slou 3B 10
Barr's Rd. SL6: Tap 5E 8
Barry Av. SL4: Wind 6B 16
Bartelotts Rd. SL2: Slou 3G 9
Bartletts La. SL6: Holy 6G 13
Barton Rd. SL3: L'ly 1A 18
Basford Way SL4: Wind 2G 21
Bassett Way SL2: Slou 3H 9
Bates Cl. SL3: G Grn 5K 11
Bath Ct. SL6: Maid 6D 6
Bath Rd. SL1: Slou 6G 9
SL3: Coln 6D 18
SL3: Coln, Poyle 7F 19
SL6: Lit G, Maid 6A 6
SL6: Tap 5K 7
UB7: Lford 7J 19
Bathurst Cl. SL0: Rich P 1G 19
Bathurst Wlk. SL0: Rich P 1F 19
Battlemead Cl. SL6: Maid 1K 7
Baxter Cl. SL1: Slou 2D 16
Bayley Cres. SL1: Burn 4D 8
Baylis Bus. Cen. SL1: Slou 6C 10
Baylis Pde. SL1: Slou 5D 10
Baylis Rd. SL1: Slou 6C 10
Bays Farm Ct. UB7: Lford 7K 19
Bay Tree Ct. SL1: Burn 2F 9
Beacon Ct. SL3: Coln 6D 18
Beaconsfield Rd. SL2: Farn C, Farn R 1B 10
Bears Rails Pk. SL4: Old Win 6E 22
Beaufort Pl. SL6: Bray 1A 14
Beauforts TW20: Eng G 4C 24
Beaulieu Cl. SL3: Dat 7G 17
Beaumaris Ct. SL2: Slou 4A 10
Beaumont Cl. SL6: Maid 2B 12
Beaumont Rd. SL2: Slou 3C 10
SL4: Wind 1B 22
Beckett Chase SL3: L'ly 4A 18
Beckwell Rd. SL1: Slou 1B 16
Bedford Av. SL1: Slou 5J 9
Bedford Cl. SL6: Maid 2B 12
Bedford Dr. SL2: Farn C 4D 4
Beeches Dr. SL2: Farn C 4D 4
Beeches Rd. SL2: Farn C 4D 4
Beechfield Pl. SL6: Maid 1D 12
Beech Rd. SL3: L'ly 1K 17
Beechtree Av. TW20: Eng G 5B 24
Beechwood Dr. SL6: Maid 6B 6
Beechwood Gdns. SL1: Slou 1D 16
Beechwood Rd. SL2: Slou 4C 10
Belfast Av. SL1: Slou 5B 10
Belgrave Pde. *SL1: Slou* *6D 10*
(off Bradley Rd.)
Belgrave Pl. SL1: Slou 1F 17
Belgrave Rd. SL1: Slou 6D 10
Bell Cl. SL2: Slou 4G 11
Bell La. SL4: Eton W 3J 15
Bell Pde. SL4: Wind 1J 21
Bellsfield Ct. *SL4: Eton W* *3J 15*
(off Bell La.)
Bells Hill SL2: Stoke P 7J 5
Bells Hill Grn. SL2: Stoke P 6J 5
Bell St. SL6: Maid 6G 7
Bell Vw. SL4: Wind 2J 21
Bell Vw. Cl. SL4: Wind 1J 21
Bell Vue Pl. SL1: Slou 2E 16
Bellweir Cl. TW19: Staines 1H 25
Belmont SL2: Slou 4K 9
Belmont Cotts. *SL3: Coln* *6D 18*
(off High St.)
Belmont Cres. SL6: Maid 4D 6
Belmont Dr. SL6: Maid 4E 6
Belmont Pk. Av. SL6: Maid 3E 6
Belmont Pk. Rd. SL6: Maid 4E 6
Belmont Rd. SL6: Maid 4E 6
Belmont Va. SL6: Maid 4E 6
Belvedere Mans. SL1: Slou 1C 16
Bembridge Ct. SL1: Slou 1E 16
Benison Ct. *SL1: Slou* *2E 16*
(off Hencroft St. Sth.)
Bennetts Cl. SL1: Slou 7K 9
Benning Cl. SL4: Wind 2G 21
Benson Cl. SL2: Slou 7F 11
Bentley Pk. SL1: Burn 1G 9
Bentley Rd. SL1: Slou 7K 9
Beresford Av. SL2: Slou 6H 11
Berkeley Cl. SL6: Maid 4B 6
TW19: Staines 1K 25
Berkeley Dr. SL4: Wink 7E 20
Berkeley M. SL1: Slou 5G 9
Berkshire Av. SL1: Slou 5A 10
Berkshire Yeomanry Mus. 3C 22
Berners Cl. SL1: Slou 6H 9
Berryfield SL2: Slou 5H 11
Berry Hill SL6: Tap 5A 8
Berwick Av. SL1: Slou 6A 10
Bessemer Cl. SL3: L'ly 4A 18
Bestobell Rd. SL1: Slou 5B 10
Beta Way TW20: Thorpe 7J 25
Bettoney Vere SL6: Bray 1K 13
Beverley Ct. SL1: Slou 1G 17
Beverley Gdns. SL6: Maid 3C 6
Bexley St. SL4: Wind 7B 16
Biddles Cl. SL1: Slou 7H 9
Bideford Spur SL2: Slou 2A 10
Bilton Cl. SL3: Poyle 7F 19
Bingham Rd. SL1: Burn 4D 8
Binghams, The SL6: Bray 2J 13
Birch Gro. SL2: Slou 4A 10
SL4: Wind 7G 15
Birchington Rd. SL4: Wind 1K 21
Birdwood Rd. SL6: Maid 5B 6
Birley Rd. SL1: Slou 5C 10
Bisham Ct. *SL1: Slou* *1E 16*
(off Park St.)
Bishop Ct. SL6: Maid 6E 6
Bishops Farm Cl. SL4: Oak G 1E 20
BISHOPS GATE 2A 24
Bishopsgate Rd. TW20: Eng G 2A 24
Bishops Orchard SL2: Farn R 2A 10
Bishops Rd. SL1: Slou 1F 17
Bishops Way TW20: Egh 5K 25
Bissley Dr. SL6: Maid 2A 12
Bix La. SL6: Maid 3A 6
Blackamoor La. SL6: Maid 3H 7
Blackbird La. SL6: Holy 7H 13

Black Horse Cl. SL4: Wind 1G 21
Black Horse Yd. SL4: Wind 7C 16
Black Lake Cl. TW20: Egh 7G 25
Black Pk. Rd. SL3: Ful, Wex 1K 11
Blackpond La. SL2: Farn C, Farn R 5D 4
Blacksmith Row SL3: L'ly 3B 18
Blackthorne Dell SL3: L'ly 2H 17
Blair Rd. SL1: Slou 7D 10
Blakeney Ct. SL6: Maid 3G 7
Blandford Cl. SL3: L'ly 2J 17
Blandford Ct. SL3: L'ly 2J 17
Blandford Rd. Nth. SL3: L'ly 2J 17
Blandford Rd. Sth. SL3: L'ly 2J 17
Blays Cl. TW20: Eng G 5C 24
Blay's La. TW20: Eng G 6B 24
Blenheim Cl. SL3: L'ly 1A 18
Blenheim Ct. TW18: Staines 3K 25
Blenheim Rd. SL3: L'ly 3J 17
SL6: Maid 4C 6
Blinco La. SL3: G Grn 5K 11
Blind La. SL6: Holy 5J 13
Blondell Cl. UB7: Harm 5K 19
Bloomfield Rd. SL6: Maid 7B 6
Blue Ball La. TW20: Egh 4F 25
Blumfield Ct. SL1: Slou 3G 9
Blumfield Cres. SL1: Slou 3G 9
Blunden Dr. SL3: L'ly 3D 18
Blythe Ho. SL1: Slou 7G 9
Boadicea Cl. SL1: Slou 7H 9
Boarlands Cl. SL1: Slou 6J 9
Boarlands Path SL1: Slou 6J 9
Bodmin Av. SL2: Slou 4K 9
Bold's Ct. SL2: Stoke P 6J 5
Bolton Av. SL4: Wind 2C 22
Bolton Cres. SL4: Wind 2B 22
Bolton Rd. SL4: Wind 2B 22
Bond St. TW20: Eng G 4B 24
Borderside SL2: Slou 5F 11
Borrowdale Cl. TW20: Egh 6H 25
Boscombe Cl. TW20: Egh 7J 25
Boshers Gdns. TW20: Egh 5F 25
Boston Gro. SL1: Slou 5B 10
Bosworth Ct. SL1: Slou 6F 9
Botham Dr. SL1: Slou 2D 16
Bottom Waltons Cvn. Site SL2: Farn R 1H 9
Boulters Cl. SL1: Slou 7K 9
SL6: Maid 3K 7
Boulters Ct. SL6: Maid 3K 7
Boulters Gdns. SL6: Maid 3K 7
Boulters La. SL6: Maid 3K 7
Boulters Lock Island SL6: Maid 2K 7
Boundary Rd. SL6: Tap 3B 8
Bourne Av. SL4: Wind 2B 22
Bourne Rd. SL1: Slou 1B 16
Bouverie Way SL3: L'ly 4K 17
BOVENEY 5G 15
Boveney Cl. SL1: Slou 1K 15
Boveney New Rd. SL4: Eton W 3H 15
Boveney Rd. SL4: Dor 3F 15
Boveney Wood La. SL1: Burn 1A 4
Bower Ct. SL1: Slou 6J 9
Bower Way SL1: Slou 6H 9
Bowes-Lyon Cl. *SL4: Wind* *7B 16*
(off Alma Rd.)
Bowes Rd. TW18: Staines 4K 25
Bowmans Cl. SL1: Burn 1E 8
Bowyer Dr. SL1: Slou 7H 9
Boyndon Rd. SL6: Maid 5E 6
BOYN HILL 6E 6
Boyn Hill Av. SL6: Maid 6E 6
Boyn Hill Cl. SL6: Maid 6E 6
Boyn Hill Rd. SL6: Maid 7D 6
Boyn Valley Ind. Est. SL6: Maid 6F 7
Boyn Valley Rd. SL6: Maid 7D 6
Bracken Cl. SL2: Farn C 3F 5
Brackenforde SL3: L'ly 1H 17
Bracken Rd. SL6: Maid 1D 12
Bradford Rd. SL1: Slou 5K 9
Bradley Rd. SL1: Slou 6C 10
Bradshaw Cl. SL4: Wind 7H 15
Braemar Gdns. SL1: Slou 1K 15
Bramber Ct. SL1: Slou 7K 9
Bramble Dr. SL6: Maid 1B 12
Brambles, The SL6: Holy 5J 13
Bramley Chase SL6: Maid 1D 12
Bramley Cl. SL6: Maid 2D 12
Brammas Cl. SL1: Slou 2B 16
Brampton Ct. SL6: Maid 4J 7
BRANDS HILL 5C 18
Brands Rd. SL3: L'ly 5C 18
BRAY 1K 13
Braybank SL6: Bray 1K 13
Bray Cl. SL6: Bray 2K 13
Bray Ct. SL6: Bray 3K 13
Brayfield Rd. SL6: Bray 1K 13
Bray Rd. SL6: Bray, Maid 6J 7
BRAY WICK 1H 13
Braywick Nature Cen. 1H 13
Braywick Rd. SL6: Bray, Maid 6G 7
Braywick Sports Cen. 7H 7
Braywood Av. TW20: Egh 5F 25
Braywood Cotts. SL4: Oak G 1D 20
Breadcroft La. SL6: Maid 2A 12
(not continuous)
Breadcroft Rd. SL6: Maid 2A 12
Brecon Ct. SL1: Slou 1B 16
Bredward Cl. SL1: Burn 2E 8
Briar Cl. SL6: Tap 5E 8
Briardene SL6: Maid 3D 6
Briars, The SL3: L'ly 4A 18
Briar Way SL2: Slou 4A 10
Brickfield La. SL1: Burn 1D 8
Bridge Av. SL6: Maid 5H 7
Bridge Cl. SL1: Slou 6J 9
TW18: Staines 3K 25
Bridgeman Ct. SL4: Wind 1K 21
Bridgeman Dr. SL4: Wind 1K 21
Bridge Rd. SL6: Maid 5H 7
Bridge St. SL3: Coln 6E 18
SL6: Maid 5H 7
Bridgewater Ct. SL3: L'ly 3B 18
Bridgewater Ter. SL4: Wind 7C 16
Bridgewater Way SL4: Wind 7C 16
Bridle Cl. SL6: Maid 3F 7
Bridle Rd. SL6: Maid 3F 7
Bridlington Spur SL1: Slou 2A 16
Bridport Way SL2: Slou 3A 10
Brighton Spur SL2: Slou 3A 10
Brill Cl. SL6: Maid 1E 12
Brinkworth Pl. SL4: Old Win 6G 23
Bristol Way SL1: Slou 7E 10
British Disabled Water-Ski Association 1H 25
BRITWELL 2K 9
Britwell Gdns. SL1: Burn 2G 9
Britwell Rd. SL1: Burn 2F 9
Broadleys SL4: Wind 6J 15
Broadmark Rd. SL2: Slou 6G 11
Broadmoor Rd. SL6: W Walt 7A 12
Broad Oak SL2: Slou 3B 10
Broad Oak Ct. SL2: Slou 3B 10
Broad Platts SL3: L'ly 2J 17
Broadwater Cl. TW19: Wray 6K 23
Broadwater Pk. SL6: Bray 4B 14
Broadway SL4: Wink 7E 20
SL6: Maid 5G 7
Broadway, The SL2: Farn C 5E 4
Brocas St. SL4: Eton 6C 16
Brocas Ter. SL4: Eton 6C 16
Brock La. SL6: Maid 5G 7
Brockton Ct. SL6: Maid 6G 7
Brockway SL3: L'ly 4C 18
Broken Furlong SL4: Eton 4A 16
Brompton Dr. SL6: Maid 3D 6
Bromycroft Rd. SL2: Slou 2K 9
Brook Cres. SL1: Slou 5H 9
Brookdene Cl. SL6: Maid 2G 7
Brook Ho. SL1: Slou 2C 16
Brook Path SL1: Slou 6J 9
(not continuous)
Brookside SL3: Coln 6D 18
Brookside Av. TW19: Wray 2K 23
Brook St. SL4: Wind 1C 22
Broom Farm Est. SL4: Wind 1F 21
Broomfield Ga. SL2: Slou 3A 10
Broom Hill SL2: Stoke P 6J 5
Broom Ho. SL3: L'ly 3A 18
Brownfield Gdns. SL6: Maid 7F 7
Browns Ct. SL1: Slou 6H 9
Bruce Cl. SL1: Slou 7K 9
Bruce Wlk. SL4: Wind 1G 21
Brudenell SL4: Wind 2J 21
Brunel Cl. SL6: Maid 7F 7
Brunel Rd. SL6: Maid 7E 6
Brunel University
Runnymede Campus 2D 24
Brunel Way SL1: Slou 7E 10
Bryant Av. SL2: Slou 4C 10
Bryer Pl. SL4: Wind 2G 21
Buccleuch Rd. SL3: Dat 6F 17
Buckfield Ct. SL0: Rich P 1G 19
Buckingham Av. SL1: Slou 5H 9
Buckingham Av. E. SL1: Slou 5B 10
Buckingham Gdns. SL1: Slou 1E 16
Buckland Av. SL3: Slou 3G 17
Buckland Cres. SL4: Wind 7J 15
Buckland Ga. SL3: Wex 2G 11
Bucklebury Cl. SL6: Holy 4K 13
Buffins SL6: Tap 2B 8
Bulkeley Av. SL4: Wind 2A 22
Bulkeley Cl. TW20: Eng G 4C 24
Bulstrode Pl. SL1: Slou 2E 16
Bunby Rd. SL2: Stoke P 6H 5
Bunce's Cl. SL4: Eton W 4A 16
Bunten Meade SL1: Slou 7A 10
Burcot Gdns. SL6: Maid 1F 7
Burfield Rd. SL4: Old Win 5F 23
Burford Gdns. SL1: Slou 4F 9
Burgett Rd. SL1: Slou 2A 16
Burlington Av. SL1: Slou 1D 16
Burlington Ct. SL1: Slou 1D 16
Burlington Rd.
SL1: Burn 3E 8
SL1: Slou 1D 16
Burnetts Rd. SL4: Wind 7H 15
BURNHAM 2F 9
BURNHAM BEECHES 4D 4
Burnham Beeches National
Nature Reserve 5B 4
Burnham Cl. SL4: Wind 1G 21
Burnham Hgts. SL1: Slou 5F 9
Burnham La. SL1: Slou 4G 9
Burnham Station (Rail) 5G 9
Burn Wlk. SL1: Burn 2E 8
Burroway Rd. SL3: L'ly 2C 18
Burton Way SL4: Wind 2H 21
Business Village, The
SL2: Slou 7G 11
Butlers Cl. SL4: Wind 7G 15
Buttermere Av. SL1: Slou 4F 9
Buttermere Way TW20: Egh 6H 25
Bybend Cl. SL2: Farn R 7D 4
Byland Dr. SL6: Holy 4J 13
Byron SL3: L'ly 4C 18
Byron Ct. SL4: Wind 2K 21
Byways SL1: Burn 4D 8

C

Caddy Cl. TW20: Egh 4G 25
Cadogan Cl. SL6: Holy 5H 13
Cadwell Dr. SL6: Maid 2E 12
Cages Wood Dr. SL2: Farn C 3D 4
Cairngorm Pl. SL2: Slou 3C 10
Calbroke Rd. SL2: Slou 3J 9
Calder Cl. SL6: Maid 3F 7
Calder Ct. SL3: L'ly 4A 18
SL6: Maid 3E 6
Callow Hill GU25: Vir W 7C 24
Cambria Ct. SL3: L'ly 1H 17
TW18: Staines 3K 25
Cambridge Av. SL1: Burn 1E 8
SL1: Slou 5K 9
Cambridge Ho. SL4: Wind 7B 16
Camden Rd. SL6: Maid 3E 6
Camley Gdns. SL6: Maid 4B 6
Camley Pk. Dr. SL6: Maid 4A 6
Camm Av. SL4: Wind 2H 21
Camperdown SL6: Maid 3J 7
Camperdown Ho. SL4: Wind 1B 22
Canada Rd. SL1: Slou 1G 17
Canadian Memorial Av. TW20: Eng G 7A 24
Canal Ind. Est. SL3: L'ly 1B 18
Canal Wharf SL3: L'ly 1B 18
Cannock Cl. SL6: Maid 6J 7
Cannon Ct. Rd. SL6: Maid 1E 6
(not continuous)
Cannon Ga. SL2: Slou 6H 11
Cannon La. SL6: Maid 6B 6
Canon Hill Cl. SL6: Bray 2J 13
Canon Hill Dr. SL6: Bray 2J 13
Canon Hill Way SL6: Bray 3J 13
Canterbury Av. SL2: Slou 3B 10
Canterbury M. SL4: Wind 1K 21
Cardigan Cl. SL1: Slou 6J 9
Cardinals Wlk. SL6: Tap 5F 9
Carey Cl. SL4: Wind 2A 22
Carisbrooke Cl. SL6: Maid 7D 6
Carisbrooke Ct. SL1: Slou 6E 10
Carlisle Rd. SL1: Slou 6C 10
Carlton Rd. SL2: Slou 6G 11
Carmarthen Rd. SL1: Slou 6D 10
Carrington Rd. SL1: Slou 6D 10
Carter Cl. SL4: Wind 1K 21
Castle Av. SL3: Dat 5F 17
Castle Ct. SL6: Maid 5E 6
Castle Dr. SL6: Maid 5E 6
Castle Farm Cvn. Site SL4: Wind 1G 21
Castle Hill SL4: Wind 7C 16
SL6: Maid 5F 7
Castle Hill Rd. TW20: Eng G 3B 24
Castle Hill Ter. SL6: Maid 5F 7
Castle M. SL6: Maid 5F 7
Castle St. SL1: Slou 2E 16
Castleview Pde. SL3: L'ly 3J 17
Castleview Rd. SL3: L'ly 3H 17
Causeway, The SL6: Bray 1J 13
(not continuous)
TW18: Staines 3J 25
Causeway Corporate Cen.
TW18: Staines 3J 25
Cavalry Cres. SL4: Wind 2B 22
Cavendish Cl. SL6: Tap 5D 8
Cavendish Ct. SL3: Poyle 7F 19

Cawcott Dr. SL4: Wind 7H **15**
Cecil Way SL2: Slou 3J **9**
Cedar Chase SL6: Tap 3A **8**
Cedar Cl. SL1: Burn 3F **9**
Cedar Ct. SL4: Wind 1K **21**
TW20: Egh 3G **25**
Cedars, The SL2: Slou 2J **9**
Cedars Rd. SL6: Maid 5H **7**
Cedar Way SL3: L'ly 4K **17**
Cell Farm Av. SL4: Old Win 4G **23**
Central Dr. SL1: Slou 6J **9**
Central La. SL4: Wink 7E **20**
Central Way SL4: Wink 7E **20**
Centre Rd. SL4: Wind 6F **15**
Century Rd. TW18: Staines 4J **25**
Chalcott SL1: Slou 2D **16**
Chalgrove Cl. SL6: Maid 6J **7**
Challow Ct. SL6: Maid 3E **6**
CHALVEY **2C 16**
Chalvey Gdns. SL1: Slou 1D **16**
Chalvey Gro. SL1: Slou 2A **16**
Chalvey Pk. SL1: Slou 1D **16**
Chalvey Rd. E. SL1: Slou 1D **16**
Chalvey Rd. W. SL1: Slou 1C **16**
Chandlers Quay SL6: Maid 5K **7**
Chandos Mall *SL1: Slou* *1E* ***16***
(off High St.)
Chandos Rd. TW18: Staines 4K **25**
Chantry Cl. SL4: Wind 7K **15**
Chapel Ct. SL6: Maid 1E **12**
Chapel La. SL2: Stoke P 6K **5**
Chapels Cl. SL1: Slou 7H **9**
Chapel St. SL1: Slou 1E **16**
Chaplin M. SL3: L'ly 4A **18**
Chapter M. SL4: Wind 6C **16**
Chariotts Pl. SL4: Wind 7C **16**
Charles Gdns. SL2: Slou 5G **11**
Charles Ho. SL4: Wind 7B **16**
Charles St. SL4: Wind 7B **16**
Charlotte Av. SL2: Slou 6E **10**
Charlton SL4: Wind 1F **21**
Charlton Cl. SL1: Slou 1A **16**
Charlton Pl. *SL4: Wind* *1F* ***21***
(off Charlton Way)
Charlton Row SL4: Wind 1F **21**
Charlton Sq. *SL4: Wind* *1F* ***21***
(off Guards Rd.)
Charlton Wlk. SL4: Wind 1F **21**
Charlton Way SL4: Wind 1F **21**
Charta Rd. TW20: Egh 4J **25**
Charter Cl. SL1: Slou 2E **16**
Charter Rd. SL1: Slou 6H **9**
Chase, The SL6: Maid 2E **6**
Chatfield SL2: Slou 4K **9**
Chatham Ct. *SL1: Slou* *2F* ***17***
(off Grove Cl.)
Chatsworth Cl. SL6: Maid 7D **6**
Chaucer Cl. SL4: Wind 2C **22**
Chaucer Way SL1: Slou 7E **10**
Chauntry Cl. SL6: Maid 6K **7**
Chauntry Rd. SL6: Maid 6J **7**
Cheniston Gro. SL6: Maid 5A **6**
Cherington Ga. SL6: Maid 3C **6**
Cherries, The SL2: Slou 5G **11**
Cherry Av. SL3: L'ly 1J **17**
Cherry Orchard SL2: Stoke P 6K **5**
Cherry Tree Rd. SL2: Farn R 6E **4**
Cherrywood Av. TW20: Eng G 6B **24**
Chertsey La. TW18: Staines 4K **25**
Cherwell Cl. SL3: L'ly 5C **18**
SL6: Maid 4H **7**
Cheshire Ct. SL1: Slou 1G **17**
Chester Rd. SL1: Slou 5C **10**
Chestnut Av. SL3: L'ly 1K **17**
Chestnut Cl. SL6: Maid 3J **7**
TW20: Eng G 5B **24**
Chestnut Dr. SL4: Wind 3H **21**
TW20: Egh 5D **24**
Chestnut Pk. SL6: Bray 3B **14**
Cheveley Gdns. SL1: Burn 1F **9**
Cheviot Cl. SL6: Maid 6J **7**
Cheviot Rd. SL3: L'ly 4B **18**
Chichester Ct. SL1: Slou 2G **17**
Chilbolton TW20: Egh 4E **24**
Chiltern Ct. *SL4: Wind* *7A* ***16***
(off Fawcett Rd.)
Chiltern Ct. M. *SL4: Wind* *7A* ***16***
(off Fawcett Rd.)
Chiltern Rd. SL1: Burn 4E **8**
SL6: Maid 6J **7**
Chilton Ct. SL6: Tap 5F **9**
Chilwick Rd. SL2: Slou 3J **9**
Christian Sq. SL4: Wind 7B **16**
Christmas La. SL2: Farn C 2E **4**
Church Cl. SL4: Eton 5C **16**
SL6: Maid 6E **6**
Church Dr. SL6: Bray 1K **13**
Churchfield M. SL2: Slou 5F **11**
Church Gro. SL3: Wex 4H **11**
Church Hill SL6: W Walt 5A **12**
Churchill Rd. SL3: L'ly 3A **18**
CHURCH LAMMAS **3K 25**
Church La. SL2: Stoke P 3E **10**
SL3: Wex 3G **11**
SL4: Wind 7C **16**
SL6: Bray 1K **13**
Church Path SL6: Bray 1K **13**
Church Rd. SL2: Farn R 2B **10**
SL4: Old Win 4G **23**
SL6: Maid 7J **7**
TW20: Egh 4F **25**
Church St. SL1: Burn 3F **9**
SL1: Slou 1B **16**
(Damson Gro.)
SL1: Slou 1E **16**
(Osborne St.)
SL4: Wind 7C **16**
TW18: Staines 3K **25**
Church Ter. SL4: Wind 1H **21**
Church Vw. SL6: W Walt 5A **12**
Church Views SL6: Maid 4G **7**
Church Wlk. SL1: Burn 3E **8**
(not continuous)
Church Wood Reserve 1G **5**
Churchyard, The SL6: Bray 1K **13**
Cineworld Cinema
Slough 1E **16**
Cinnamon Cl. SL4: Wind 7J **15**
CIPPENHAM **6H 9**
Cippenham Cl. SL1: Slou 6J **9**
Cippenham La. SL1: Slou 6J **9**
Clandon Av. TW20: Egh 6J **25**
Clappers Mdw. SL6: Maid 3J **7**
Clare Dr. SL2: Farn C 3D **4**
Clarefield Cl. SL6: Maid 3B **6**
Clarefield Dr. SL6: Maid 3B **6**
Clarefield Rd. SL6: Maid 3C **6**
Clare Gdns. TW20: Egh 4G **25**
Claremont Rd. SL4: Wind 1B **22**
TW18: Staines 4K **25**
Clarence Ct. SL4: Wind 7A **16**
TW20: Egh *4F* ***25***
(off Clarence St.)
Clarence Cres. SL4: Wind 7B **16**
Clarence Dr. TW20: Eng G 3C **24**
Clarence Rd. SL4: Wind 1K **21**
Clarence St. TW20: Egh 5F **25**
Clarendon Ct. SL2: Slou 6G **11**
SL4: Wind 7A **16**
Clare Rd. SL6: Maid 6E **6**
SL6: Tap 5F **9**
Clayhall La. SL4: Old Win 4E **22**
(not continuous)
Clayton Ct. SL3: L'ly 2B **18**
Cleares Pasture SL1: Burn 2E **8**
Clements Cl. SL1: Slou 1G **17**
Clevehurst Cl. SL2: Stoke P 5J **5**
Cleveland Cl. SL6: Maid 6J **7**
Cleves Ct. SL4: Wind 2J **21**
Clewer Av. SL4: Wind 1K **21**
Clewer Ct. Rd. SL4: Wind 6A **16**
Clewer Flds. SL4: Wind 7B **16**
CLEWER GREEN **1J 21**
CLEWER HILL **2H 21**
Clewer Hill Rd. SL4: Wind 1H **21**
CLEWER NEW TOWN **1A 22**
Clewer New Town SL4: Wind 1K **21**
Clewer Pk. SL4: Wind 6K **15**
CLEWER ST ANDREW **6K 15**
CLEWER ST STEPHEN **6A 16**
CLEWER VILLAGE **7K 15**
CLEWER WITHIN **7B 16**
Clifton Cl. SL6: Bray 1H **13**
Clifton Lodge SL4: Eton W 4K **15**
Clifton Ri. SL4: Wind 7G **15**
Clifton Rd. SL1: Slou 1G **17**
Clive Ct. SL1: Slou 1C **16**
Cliveden Mead SL6: Maid 2J **7**
Cliveden Rd. SL6: Tap 3A **8**
Clivemont Rd. SL6: Maid 3G **7**
Clockhouse La. E. TW20: Egh 6H **25**
Clockhouse La. W. TW20: Egh 6G **25**
Cloisters, The SL1: Slou 1C **16**
Clonmel Way SL1: Burn 2E **8**
Close, The SL1: Slou 6G **9**
Coachmans Lodge *SL4: Wind* *1C* ***22***
(off Frances Rd.)
Coalmans Way SL1: Burn 4D **8**
Cobb Cl. SL3: Dat 7J **17**
Cobblers Cl. SL2: Farn R 1A **10**
Cobham Cl. SL1: Slou 1J **15**
Cockett Rd. SL3: L'ly 2K **17**
Coe Spur SL1: Slou 1A **16**
Coftards SL2: Slou 5H **11**
Colenorton Cres. SL4: Eton W 3H **15**
Coleridge Cres. SL3: Poyle 7F **19**
Colin Way SL1: Slou 2A **16**
College Av. SL1: Slou 2D **16**
SL6: Maid 5F **7**
TW20: Egh 5H **25**
College Cres. SL4: Wind 1A **22**
College Glen SL6: Maid 5E **6**
College Ri. SL6: Maid 5E **6**
College Rd. SL1: Slou 7J **9**
SL6: Maid 4E **6**
Colley Hill La. SL2: Hedg 2H **5**
Collier Cl. SL6: Maid 3G **7**
Collinswood Rd. SL2: Farn C 1C **4**
Collum Grn. Rd.
SL2: Farn C, Hedg, Stoke P 2F **5**
COLNBROOK **6E 18**
Colnbrook By-Pass SL3: Coln, L'ly 5D **18**
UB7: Harm 6J **19**
Colnbrook Ct. SL3: Poyle 7G **19**
Coln Cl. SL6: Maid 4G **7**
Colndale Rd. SL3: Poyle 7F **19**
Colne Av. UB7: W Dray 1K **19**
Colne Pk. Cvn. Site UB7: W Dray 3K **19**
Colne Way TW19: Staines 1H **25**
Coln Trad. Est. SL3: Poyle 7G **19**
Colonial Rd. SL1: Slou 1F **17**
Combermere Cl. SL4: Wind 1A **22**
Common, The UB7: W Dray 3K **19**
Common La. SL4: Eton 4B **16**
Common Rd. SL3: L'ly 3B **18**
SL4: Dor, Eton W 3F **15**
SL4: Eton W 4J **15**
Common Wood SL2: Farn C 3E **4**
Compton Ct. SL1: Slou 5H **9**
Compton Dr. SL6: Maid 4B **6**
Concorde Ct. SL4: Wind 1K **21**
Concorde Rd. SL6: Maid 1E **12**
Concorde Way SL1: Slou 1B **16**
Conduit La. SL3: L'ly 5K **17**
Conegar Ct. SL1: Slou 7D **10**
Conifer La. TW20: Egh 4J **25**
Conifer Wlk. SL4: Wind 6F **15**
Coningsby Cl. SL6: Maid 2E **12**
Coningsby La. SL6: Fifi 7K **13**
Coniston Cres. SL1: Slou 4F **9**
Coniston Way TW20: Egh 6H **25**
Connaught Cl. SL6: Maid 3F **7**
Connaught Rd. SL1: Slou 1G **17**
Convent Rd. SL4: Wind 1J **21**
Conway Rd. SL6: Tap 5E **8**
Cookham Rd. SL6: Maid 2F **7**
Coombe Hill Ct. SL4: Wind 2G **21**
Coopers Hill La. TW20: Egh, Eng G 2C **24**
(not continuous)
Cooper Way SL1: Slou 2A **16**
Cope Ct. SL6: Maid 5D **6**
Copper Beech Cl. SL4: Wind 7G **15**
Copperfield Ter. *SL2: Slou* *6G* ***11***
(off Mirador Cres.)
SL2: Slou *6G* ***11***
(off Mirador Cres.)
Coppice Dr. TW19: Wray 6J **23**
Coppice Way SL2: Hedg 1F **5**
Copse, The SL4: Wink 7D **20**
Copse Cl. SL1: Slou 7J **9**
UB7: W Dray 2K **19**
Copthorn Cl. SL6: Maid 1B **12**
Corby Cl. TW20: Eng G 5C **24**
Corby Dr. TW20: Eng G 5B **24**
Cordwallis Pk. SL6: Maid 4F **7**
Cordwallis Rd. SL6: Maid 4F **7**
Cordwallis St. SL6: Maid 4F **7**
Corfe Gdns. SL1: Slou 6K **9**
Corfe Pl. SL6: Maid 5D **6**
Cornel Ho. SL4: Wind 2C **22**
Cornwall Av. SL2: Slou 3B **10**
Cornwall Cl. SL4: Eton W 4H **15**
SL6: Maid 2F **7**
Cornwell Rd. SL4: Old Win 5F **23**
Coronation Av. SL3: G Grn 4K **11**
SL4: Wind 1F **23**
Cotswold Cl. SL1: Slou 2B **16**
SL6: Maid 6J **7**
Cottage Pk. Rd. SL2: Hedg 1F **5**
Cottesbrooke Cl. SL3: Coln 7E **18**
Coulson Way SL1: Burn 4E **8**
Court Cl. SL6: Bray 3K **13**
Court Cres. SL1: Slou 5C **10**
Court Dr. SL6: Maid 1K **7**
Court Farm Ho. SL1: Slou 7A **10**
Courtfield Dr. SL6: Maid 6D **6**
Courthouse Rd. SL6: Maid 5D **6**
Courtlands SL6: Maid 6G **7**
Courtlands Av. SL3: L'ly 3J **17**
Court La. SL0: Iver 1H **19**
(not continuous)
SL1: Burn 2G **9**
SL4: Dor 2D **14**
Court Rd. SL6: Maid 2K **7**

Courtyard, The SL3: L'ly 1B 18
Coverdale Way SL2: Slou 3H 9
Cowper Rd. SL2: Slou 3K 9
COX GREEN 2C 12
Cox Grn. La. SL6: Maid 2C 12
Cox Grn. Rd. SL6: Maid 1D 12
Crabtree Office Village TW20: Thorpe 7J 25
Crabtree Rd. TW20: Thorpe 7J 25
Crambourne Av. SL4: Wind 1J 21
CRANBOURNE 7E 20
Cranbourne Cl. SL1: Slou 7B 10
Cranbourne Hall Cvn. Site SL4: Wink 7D 20
Cranbourne Hall Cotts. SL4: Wink 7E 20
Cranbourne Rd. SL1: Slou 7B 10
Cranbrook Dr. SL6: Maid 3C 6
Craufurd Ct. SL6: Maid 4F 7
Craufurd Ri. SL6: Maid 4F 7
Crayle St. SL2: Slou 2K 9
Creden Cl. SL6: Maid 3E 6
Crescent, The SL1: Slou 1D 16
(not continuous)
SL6: Maid 5F 7
TW20: Egh 5E 24
Crescent Dale SL6: Maid 6G 7
Crescent Dr. SL6: Maid 5F 7
Cress Rd. SL1: Slou 1A 16
Cresswells Mead SL6: Holy 4J 13
Cricketfield Rd. UB7: W Dray 3K 19
Crimp Hill SL4: Eng G, Old Win 6E 22
TW20: Eng G 2A 24
Crispin Way SL2: Farn C 3F 5
Croft, The SL6: Maid 7D 6
Croft Cnr. SL4: Old Win 4G 23
Crofters SL4: Old Win 5F 23
Crofthill Rd. SL2: Slou 3A 10
Cromer Ct. SL1: Slou 5D 10
Cromwell Dr. SL1: Slou 5D 10
Cromwell Rd. SL6: Maid 5E 6
Cromwells Ct. SL3: L'ly 7K 11
Cross Oak SL4: Wind 1K 21
Crossways TW20: Egh 5K 25
Crossways Ct. SL4: Wind 1B 22
(off Osbourne Rd.)
Crosthwaite Way SL1: Slou 4G 9
Crouch La. SL4: Wink 6B 20
Crown Cl. SL3: Coln 6D 18
Crown Cotts. SL4: Wind 3C 22
Crown La. SL2: Farn R 1K 9
SL6: Maid 5H 7
Crown Mdw. SL3: Coln 6C 18
Crown St. TW20: Egh 3G 25
Crow Piece La. SL2: Farn R 6B 4
(not continuous)
Croxley Ri. SL6: Maid 6E 6
Crummock Cl. SL1: Slou 5F 9
Culham Dr. SL6: Maid 2F 7
Cullerns Pas. SL6: Maid 6G 7
Culley Way SL6: Maid 1B 12
Cumberland Av. SL2: Slou 3B 10
Cumberland St. TW18: Staines 4K 25
Cumbrae Cl. SL2: Slou 7F 11
Cumbria Cl. SL6: Maid 1D 12
Curfew Yd. SL4: Wind 6C 16
Curls La. SL6: Maid 1F 13
Curls Rd. SL6: Maid 1E 12
Curriers La. SL1: Burn 4A 4
Curzon Mall SL1: Slou 1E 16
(off Wellington St.)
Cut, The SL2: Slou 3K 9
Cypress Ho. SL3: L'ly 4C 18
Cypress Wlk. TW20: Eng G 5B 24

D

Dagmar Rd. SL4: Wind 1C 22
Dairy Ct. SL6: Holy 6H 13
Daisy Mdw. TW20: Egh 4G 25
Dale Ct. SL1: Slou 1B 16
Daleham Av. TW20: Egh 5G 25
Dalton Grn. SL3: L'ly 5A 18
Damson Gro. SL1: Slou 1B 16
Dandridge Cl. SL3: L'ly 3J 17
Danehurst Cl. TW20: Egh 5E 24
Darkhole Ride SL4: Wink 3D 20
Darling's La. SL6: Maid 4A 6
Darrell Cl. SL3: L'ly 3A 18
Dart Cl. SL3: L'ly 4C 18
Darvill's La. SL1: Slou 1C 16
Darwin Rd. SL3: L'ly 1A 18
Dashwood Cl. SL3: L'ly 3H 17
DATCHET 6G 17
DATCHET COMMON 7J 17
Datchet Pl. SL3: Dat 7G 17
Datchet Rd. SL3: Hort 2K 23
SL3: Slou 3E 16
SL4: Old Win 3F 23
SL4: Wind 6C 16
Datchet Station (Rail) 7G 17
Daventry Cl. SL3: Poyle 7G 19
David Lloyd Leisure
Maidenhead 6G 7
Davison Rd. SL3: L'ly 4A 18
Dawes E. Rd. SL1: Burn 3F 9
Dawes Moor Cl. SL2: Slou 5H 11
Dawley Ride SL3: Poyle 7F 19
Dawson Cl. SL4: Wind 1K 21
Deacon Ct. SL4: Wind 1G 21
Deal Av. SL1: Slou 5J 9
Dean Cl. SL4: Wind 2G 21
Deans Cl. SL2: Stoke P 7K 5
Deansfield Cl. SL6: Maid 2E 6
Decies Way SL2: Stoke P 7J 5
DEDWORTH 1H 21
Dedworth Dr. SL4: Wind 7J 15
DEDWORTH GREEN 2G 21
Dedworth Mnr. SL4: Wind 7J 15
Dedworth Rd. SL4: Wind 1F 21
Deena Cl. SL1: Slou 6H 9
Deep Fld. SL3: Dat 6G 17
Dee Rd. SL4: Wind 6F 15
Deerswood SL6: Maid 3H 7
Dell, The SL6: Maid 2A 12
TW20: Eng G 2A 24
Dell Cl. SL2: Farn C 4E 4
Delta Way TW20: Thorpe 7J 25
Denham Cl. SL6: Maid 6D 6
Denham Rd. TW20: Egh 3G 25
Denmark St. SL6: Maid 4F 7
Dennis Way SL1: Slou 6G 9
Denny Rd. SL3: L'ly 3A 18
Depot Rd. SL6: Maid 6G 7
Derek Rd. SL6: Maid 4K 7
De Ros Pl. TW20: Egh 5G 25
Derwent Dr. SL1: Slou 4F 9
SL6: Maid 4E 6
Derwent Rd. TW20: Egh 6H 25
Desborough Cres. SL6: Maid 7D 6
Deseronto Trad. Est. SL3: L'ly 1K 17
Devereux Rd. SL4: Wind 1C 22
Deverills Way SL3: L'ly 3D 18
Devil's La. TW18: Staines 6K 25
TW20: Egh 5J 25
Devon Av. SL1: Slou 5B 10
Devonshire Cl. SL2: Farn R 1A 10
Devonshire Grn. SL2: Farn R 1A 10
Dewar Spur SL3: L'ly 5A 18
Dhoon Ri. SL6: Maid 6G 7
Diamond Rd. SL1: Slou 1F 17
Diana Cl. SL3: G Grn 5K 11
Dickens Pl. SL3: Poyle 7F 19
Dimsdale Dr. SL2: Farn C 4A 4
Disraeli Ct. SL3: L'ly 5C 18
Ditton Pk. Rd. SL3: L'ly 5K 17
Ditton Rd. SL3: Dat 7J 17
SL3: L'ly 4A 18
Doddsfield Rd. SL2: Slou 2K 9
Dolphin Ct. SL1: Slou 1G 17
Dolphin Rd. SL1: Slou 1G 17
Donkey La. UB7: W Dray 3K 19
Donnington Gdns. SL6: Maid 3G 7
Dorchester Cl. SL6: Maid 3C 6
Dornels SL2: Slou 5H 11
DORNEY 2E 14
Dorney Court 2E 14
Dorney Lake Rowing Cen. 6G 15
DORNEY REACH 2C 14
Dorney Reach Rd. SL6: Dor R 2C 14
Dorney Wood Rd. SL1: Burn 3A 4 & 1F 9
Dorset Rd. SL4: Wind 1B 22
Douglas Rd. SL2: Slou 4C 10
Dove Ho. Cres. SL2: Slou 2H 9
Dover Rd. SL1: Slou 5J 9
Dower Pk. SL4: Wind 3H 21
Downing Path SL2: Slou 3H 9
Down Pl. SL4: Wat O 5D 14
Downs Rd. SL3: L'ly 1J 17
Dragons Health Club 5H 9
(off Bunrham La.)
Drake Av. SL3: L'ly 3J 17
Drew Mdw. SL2: Farn C 3E 4
Drift Rd. SL4: Wink 3A 20
Drift Way SL3: Coln 7D 18
Drive, The SL3: Dat 7G 17
SL3: L'ly 1K 17
TW19: Wray 4J 23
Dropmore Rd. SL1: Burn 1F 9
Drummond Ho. SL4: Wind 2C 22
(off Balmoral Gdns.)
Duchess St. SL1: Slou 7H 9
Dudley Ct. SL1: Slou 2F 17
Duffield La. SL2: Stoke P 5H 5
Duffield Pk. SL2: Stoke P 2F 11
Dugdale Ho. TW20: Egh 4J 25
(off Pooley Grn. Rd.)
Dukes Dr. SL2: Farn C 4B 4
Dukes Kiln Dr. SL9: Ger X 1K 5
Duke St. SL4: Wind 6B 16
Dukes Valley SL9: Ger X 1K 5
Dunbar Cl. SL2: Slou 6F 11
Duncannon Cres. SL4: Wind 2G 21
Duncroft SL4: Wind 2J 21
Duncroft Mnr. TW18: Staines 3K 25
Dundee Rd. SL1: Slou 5J 9
Dungrove Hill La. SL6: Maid 1A 6
Dunholme End SL6: Maid 2E 12
Dunster Gdns. SL1: Slou 6K 9
Dunwood Ct. SL6: Maid 7D 6
Dupre Cl. SL1: Slou 1H 15
Durham Av. SL1: Slou 5K 9
Dutch Elm Av. SL4: Wind 6E 16
Dyson Cl. SL4: Wind 2A 22

E

Earlsfield SL6: Holy 4K 13
Earls La. SL1: Slou 7J 9
Eastbourne Rd. SL1: Slou 5K 9
Eastbridge SL1: Slou 1G 17
EAST BURNHAM 6C 4
E. Burnham La. SL2: Farn R 7C 4
East Cres. SL4: Wind 7J 15
Eastcroft SL2: Slou 3A 10
East Dr. SL2: Stoke P 2D 10
Eastfield Cl. SL1: Slou 2F 17
Eastfield Rd. SL1: Burn 4D 8
East Rd. SL6: Maid 5F 7
East Ter. SL4: Wind 7D 16
Ebsworth Cl. SL6: Maid 1K 7
Eden Cl. SL3: L'ly 4B 18
Edinburgh Av. SL1: Slou 4K 9
Edinburgh Gdns. SL4: Wind 1C 22
Edinburgh Rd. SL6: Maid 3F 7
Edith Rd. SL6: Maid 5B 6
Edmunds Way SL2: Slou 4G 11
Edwards Ct. SL1: Slou 1D 16
Egerton Rd. SL2: Slou 3H 9
EGHAM 4G 25
Egham Bus. Village TW20: Thorpe 7J 25
Egham By-Pass TW20: Egh 4F 25
Egham Hill TW20: Egh, Eng G 5D 24
EGHAM HYTHE 5K 25
Egham Mus. 4G 25
Egham Rdbt. TW18: Staines 4K 25
Egham Sports Cen. 5H 25
Egham Station (Rail) 4G 25
EGHAM WICK 6A 24
Egremont Gdns. SL1: Slou 7K 9
EGYPT 3D 4
Egypt La. SL2: Farn C 1D 4
Eight Acres SL1: Burn 3E 8
Elbow Mdw. SL3: Poyle 7G 19
Elderfield Rd. SL2: Stoke P 5H 5
Elder Way SL3: L'ly 1A 18
Elizabeth Ct. SL1: Slou 1F 17
SL4: Wind 1B 22
(off St Leonard's Rd.)
Elizabeth Way SL2: Stoke P 7H 5
Elkins Rd. SL2: Hedg 1G 5
Ellesmere Cl. SL3: Dat 5F 17
Elliman Av. SL2: Slou 6D 10
Elliman Sq. SL1: Slou 1E 16
(off High St.)
Ellington Ct. SL6: Tap 5K 7
Ellington Gdns. SL6: Tap 5K 7
Ellington Pk. SL6: Maid 3F 7
Ellington Rd. SL6: Tap 5K 7
Ellis Av. SL1: Slou 1D 16
Ellison Cl. SL4: Wind 2J 21
Ellison Ho. SL4: Wind 7C 16
(off Victoria St.)
Elmar Grn. SL2: Slou 2K 9
Elmbank Av. TW20: Eng G 5B 24
Elm Cl. SL2: Farn C 5E 4
Elm Cft. SL3: Dat 7H 17
Elm Dr. SL4: Wink 7E 20
Elm Gro. SL6: Maid 5F 7
Elmhurst Rd. SL3: L'ly 2B 18
Elm Rd. SL4: Wind 2A 22
Elmshott La. SL1: Slou 6H 9
Elmwood SL6: Maid 1J 7
Elmwood Rd. SL2: Slou 6G 11
Elruge Cl. UB7: W Dray 2K 19
Eltham Av. SL1: Slou 1H 15
Elton Dr. SL6: Maid 4E 6
Elwell Cl. TW20: Egh 5G 25
Ely Av. SL1: Slou 4B 10
Embankment, The TW19: Wray 6H 23
Ember Rd. SL3: L'ly 2C 18
Emerald Ct. SL1: Slou 1D 16
Emilia Cl. SL6: Maid 3G 7
Emlyn Bldgs. SL4: Eton 6B 16
Englefield Cl. TW20: Eng G 5C 24

ENGLEFIELD GREEN 4C 24
Englehurst TW20: Eng G 5C 24
English Gdns. TW19: Wray 3J 23
Ennerdale Cres. SL1: Slou 4F 9
Erica Cl. SL1: Slou 6H 9
Errington Dr. SL4: Wind 7K 15
Eschle Ct. SL2: Slou 5D 10
Eskdale Gdns. SL6: Holy 3J 13
Essex Av. SL2: Slou 4B 10
ETON 5C 16
Eton Cl. SL3: Dat 5F 17
Eton College 5C 16
Eton Ct. SL4: Eton 6C 16
Eton Riverside SL4: Eton 6C 16
Eton Rd. SL3: Dat 4E 16
Eton Sq. SL4: Eton 6C 16
Eton Wlk. *SL1: Slou* *2D 16*
(off Upton Pk.)
ETON WICK 3J 15
Eton Wick Rd. SL4: Eton W 3H 15
Evenlode SL6: Maid 4G 7
Everard Av. SL1: Slou 1D 16
Evergreen Oak Av. SL4: Wind 2F 23
Eversley Way TW20: Thorpe 7J 25
Eyre Grn. SL2: Slou 2K 9

F

Fair Acre SL6: Maid 6D 6
Fairacres Ind. Est. SL4: Wind 1F 21
Faircroft SL2: Slou 3A 10
Fairfield App. TW19: Wray 5J 23
Fairfield Av. SL3: Dat 6H 17
Fairfield Cl. SL3: Dat 6J 17
Fairfield La. SL2: Farn R 1A 10
Fairfield Rd. SL1: Burn 2F 9
TW19: Wray 5J 23
Fairford Rd. SL6: Maid 4G 7
Fairhaven TW20: Egh 4F 25
Fairhaven Ct. TW20: Egh 4F 25
Fairlawn Pk. SL4: Wind 3H 21
Fairlea SL6: Maid 1B 12
Fairlie Rd. SL1: Slou 5K 9
Fairlight Av. SL4: Wind 1C 22
Fairview Rd. SL2: Slou 3J 9
SL6: Tap 5D 8
Fairway, The SL1: Burn 1F 9
SL6: Maid 2C 12
Fairway Av. UB7: W Dray 1K 19
Falaise TW20: Egh 4E 24
Falconwood TW20: Egh 4E 24
Fallows, The SL6: Maid 3H 7
Falmouth Rd. SL1: Slou 5K 9
Fane Way SL6: Maid 1E 12
Faraday Cl. SL2: Slou 4A 10
Faraday Rd. SL2: Slou 4A 10
Farm Cl. SL6: Holy 4K 13
SL6: Maid 5B 6
SL6: Tap 5D 8
Farm Cres. SL2: Slou 4G 11
Farm Dr. SL4: Old Win 5G 23
Farmers Cl. SL6: Maid 1B 12
Farmers Rd. TW18: Staines 4K 25
Farmers Way SL6: Maid 7B 6
Farm La. SL1: Slou 6C 10
Farm Rd. SL6: Maid 5B 6
SL6: Tap 5D 8
Farm Yd. SL4: Wind 6C 16
Farnburn Av. SL1: Slou 4A 10
FARNHAM COMMON 5E 4
Farnham La. SL2: Slou 2H 9
Farnham Pk. La. SL2: Farn R 6E 4
Farnham Rd. SL1: Slou 2A 10
SL2: Farn R, Slou 2A 10
FARNHAM ROYAL 2B 10
Farthingales, The SL6: Maid 5J 7
Farthing Grn. La. SL2: Stoke P 1F 11
Fawcett Rd. SL4: Wind 7A 16
Fawley Cl. SL6: Maid 2E 6
Fawsley Cl. SL3: Poyle 6F 19
Feathers La. TW19: Wray 1G 25
Ferndale Pk. SL6: Bray 5B 14
Fern Dr. SL6: Tap 5E 8
Fernley Ct. SL6: Maid 3E 6
Ferrers Cl. SL1: Slou 7H 9
Ferry La. TW19: Wray 1H 25
Ferry Rd. SL6: Bray 1K 13
Fetty Pl. SL6: Maid 1E 12
Fieldhurst SL3: L'ly 4A 18
Fielding Gdns. SL3: L'ly 1H 17
Fielding Rd. SL6: Maid 5C 6
Fieldings, The SL6: Holy 6H 13
Fields, The SL1: Slou 1C 16
Field Vw. TW20: Egh 4J 25
FIFIELD 7A 14
Fifield La. SL4: Wink 3A 20
Fifield Rd. SL6: Bray, Fifi 6A 14
Filey Spur SL1: Slou 1A 16
Filmer Rd. SL4: Wind 1G 21
Finch Ct. SL6: Maid 7E 6
Firbank Pl. TW20: Eng G 5B 24
Fircroft Cl. SL2: Stoke P 5J 5
Firs Av. SL4: Wind 2J 21
Firs Dr. SL3: L'ly 7K 11
Firs La. SL6: Maid 1A 12
First Cres. SL1: Slou 4B 10
Fir Tree Av. SL2: Stoke P 3E 10
FISHERY 6J 7
Fishery Rd. SL6: Maid 7J 7
Fishguard Spur SL1: Slou 1G 17
Fitzrobert Pl. TW20: Egh 5G 25
Flamborough Spur SL1: Slou 1K 15
Flanders Ct. TW20: Egh 4J 25
Fleetbrook Ho. SL3: Dat 7J 17
Fleetwood Rd. SL2: Slou 7E 10
Florence Av. SL6: Maid 4G 7
Foliejohn Way SL6: Maid 3A 12
Folkestone Ct. SL3: L'ly 4B 18
Follett Cl. SL4: Old Win 5G 23
Folly Way SL6: Maid 5F 7
Fontwell Cl. SL6: Maid 4A 6
Forbe's Ride SL4: Wink 5D 20
Forest Grn. Rd. SL6: Fifi, Holy 7F 13
Forest Rd. SL4: Wind 1G 21
(Ash La.)
SL4: Wind 7G 21
(Plain Ride)
Forge Dr. SL2: Farn C 5E 4
Forlease Cl. SL6: Maid 6H 7
Forlease Dr. SL6: Maid 6H 7
Forlease Rd. SL6: Maid 5H 7
Formby Cl. SL3: L'ly 3D 18
Forsythia Gdns. SL3: L'ly 2K 17
Foster Av. SL4: Wind 2H 21
Fosters Path SL2: Slou 3J 9
Fotherby Ct. SL6: Maid 6H 7
Fotheringay Gdns. SL1: Slou 6K 9
Fountain Gdns. SL4: Wind 2C 22
Foxborough Cl. SL3: L'ly 4B 18
Foxborough Ct. SL6: Maid 1F 13
Foxherne SL3: L'ly 1H 17
Foxhollow Dr. SL2: Farn C 4E 4
Fox Rd. SL3: L'ly 3J 17
Frances Av. SL6: Maid 3K 7
Frances Rd. SL4: Wind 2B 22
Francis Way SL1: Slou 6G 9
Franklin Av. SL2: Slou 3A 10
Franklyn Cres. SL4: Wind 2G 21
Frank Sutton Way SL1: Slou 6C 10
Frascati Way SL6: Maid 5G 7
Fratons, The SL6: Maid 5B 6
Frays Av. UB7: W Dray 1K 19
Frays Cl. UB7: W Dray 2K 19
Freemans Cl. SL2: Stoke P 5H 5
Freestone Yd. *SL3: Coln* *6E 18*
(off Park St.)
Frenchum Gdns. SL1: Slou 7H 9
Frensham Wlk. SL2: Farn C 4E 4
Friary, The SL4: Old Win 5H 23
FRIARY ISLAND 5H 23
Friary Island TW19: Wray 5H 23
Friary Rd. TW19: Wray 6H 23
(not continuous)
Frithe, The SL2: Slou 5G 11
FROGMORE 2E 22
Frogmore Border SL4: Wind 2D 22
Frogmore Cl. SL1: Slou 1K 15
Frogmore Dr. SL4: Wind 7D 16
Frogmore House 2E 22
Frymley Vw. SL4: Wind 7G 15
Fullbrook Cl. SL6: Maid 4H 7
Furness SL4: Wind 1F 21
Furness Pl. SL4: Wind 1F 21
Furness Row SL4: Wind 1F 21
Furness Sq. SL4: Wind 1F 21
Furness Wlk. *SL4: Wind* *1F 21*
(off Furnace Sq.)
Furness Way SL4: Wind 1F 21
Furnival Av. SL2: Slou 4A 10
Furrow Way SL6: Maid 1B 12
Furzedown Cl. TW20: Egh 5E 24
Furzen Cl. SL2: Slou 2K 9
FURZE PLATT 2E 6
Furze Platt Rd. SL6: Maid 2B 6
Furze Platt Station (Rail) 3F 7
Furze Rd. SL6: Maid 3E 6
Fuzzens Wlk. SL4: Wind 1H 21

G

Gables Cl. SL3: Dat 5F 17
SL6: Maid 4J 7
Gage Cl. SL6: Maid 1F 13
Gainsborough Dr. SL6: Maid 2E 12
Gala Bingo
Slough 1D 16
Galahad Cl. SL1: Slou 1K 15
Galleons La. SL3: Wex 3H 11
(not continuous)
Galleymead Rd. SL3: Poyle 7G 19
Gallop, The SL4: Wind 6B 22
Galloway Chase SL2: Slou 6F 11
Gallys Rd. SL4: Wind 1G 21
Galvin Rd. SL1: Slou 7B 10
Garden Cl. SL6: Maid 7B 6
Garden M. SL1: Slou 7E 10
Gardner Ho. SL6: Maid 3F 7
Gardner Rd. SL6: Maid 2E 6
Garfield Pl. SL4: Wind 1C 22
Garnet Cl. SL1: Slou 1K 15
Garrard Rd. SL2: Slou 3H 9
Garson La. TW19: Wray 6J 23
Garthlands SL6: Maid 2E 6
Gascon's Gro. SL2: Slou 3K 9
Gas La. SL6: Bray 2H 13
Gatehouse Cl. SL4: Wind 3A 22
Gatewick Cl. SL1: Slou 7D 10
Gatward Av. SL6: Maid 2C 12
Gaveston Rd. SL2: Slou 2J 9
Gays La. SL6: Holy 6J 13
GEORGE GREEN 5K 11
George Grn. Dr. SL3: G Grn 5K 11
George Grn. Rd. SL3: G Grn 5J 11
Gerrards Cross Rd. SL2: Stoke P 5J 5
Gervaise Cl. SL1: Slou 7J 9
Gibson Ct. SL3: L'ly 4A 18
Gilbert Way SL3: L'ly 4A 18
Gilliat Rd. SL1: Slou 6D 10
Gilman Cres. SL4: Wind 2G 21
Gilmore Cl. SL3: L'ly 1H 17
Gladstone Ind. Est. *SL6: Maid* *4F 7*
(off Denmark St.)
Gladstone Way SL1: Slou 7K 9
Glanmor Rd. SL2: Slou 6G 11
GLANTY 3J 25
Glanty, The TW20: Egh 3H 25
Glebe Cl. SL6: Tap 7C 8
Glebe Rd. SL4: Old Win 4G 23
SL6: Maid 7J 7
TW20: Egh 4J 25
Glen, The SL3: L'ly 3H 17
Glenavon Gdns. SL3: L'ly 3H 17
Glenfields SL2: Stoke P 7H 5
Glentworth Pl. SL1: Slou 7B 10
Gloucester Av. SL1: Slou 4B 10
Gloucester Dr. TW18: Staines 2J 25
Gloucester Pl. SL4: Wind 1C 22
Gloucester Rd. SL6: Maid 2F 7
Godolphin Rd. SL1: Slou 6C 10
Golden Ball La. SL6: Maid 1B 6
Golden Oak Cl. SL2: Farn C 5E 4
Goldsworthy Way SL1: Slou 5F 9
Goodman Pk. SL2: Slou 7H 11
Goodwin Rd. SL2: Slou 2J 9
Goose Grn. SL2: Farn R 1A 10
Gordon Rd. SL4: Wind 1J 21
SL6: Maid 5E 6
TW18: Staines 3J 25
Gore, The SL1: Burn 2D 8
Gore Rd. SL1: Burn 2E 8
Goring Rd. TW18: Staines 4K 25
Gorse Meade SL1: Slou 7A 10
Goslar Way SL4: Wind 1A 22
Gosling Grn. SL3: L'ly 2K 17
Gosling Rd. SL3: L'ly 2K 17
Goswell Hill SL4: Wind 7C 16
Goswell Rd. SL4: Wind 7C 16
Gowings Grn. SL1: Slou 1H 15
Grace Ct. SL1: Slou 7B 10
Grafton Cl. SL3: G Grn 5K 11
SL6: Maid 2F 7
Graham Cl. SL6: Maid 7D 6
Grampian Way SL3: L'ly 4B 18
Grange, The *SL1: Burn* *2F 9*
(off Green La.)
SL4: Old Win 4G 23
Grange Cl. TW19: Wray 5K 23
Grange Ct. TW20: Egh 4F 25
Grange Gdns. SL2: Farn C 4F 5
Grange Rd. TW20: Egh 4F 25
(not continuous)
Grangewood SL3: Wex 4H 11
Grant Av. SL1: Slou 5D 10
Granville Av. SL2: Slou 4C 10
Grasholm Way SL3: L'ly 3D 18
Grasmere SL4: Wind 6H 15
Grasmere Av. SL2: Slou 6F 11
Grasmere Cl. TW20: Egh 6H 25
Grasmere Pde. SL2: Slou 6G 11
Grassy La. SL6: Maid 5F 7
Gratton Dr. SL4: Wind 3H 21
Grays All. SL6: Maid 5A 6

Grays Pk. Rd. SL2: Stoke P 1F 11
Grays Pl. SL2: Slou 7E 10
Gray's Rd. SL1: Slou 7E 10
Gt. Hill Cres. SL6: Maid 7C 6
Green, The SL1: Burn 4E 8
SL1: Slou 1C 16
SL3: Dat 6G 17
TW19: Wray 5K 23
TW20: Eng G 3C 24
Greenacre SL4: Wind 1H 21
Greenacre Ct. TW20: Eng G 5C 24
Green Bus. Cen., The
TW18: Staines 3J 25
Green Cl. SL6: Maid 3G 7
SL6: Tap 5D 8
Greendale M. SL2: Slou 6F 11
Green Dr. SL3: L'ly 3K 17
(not continuous)
SL6: Tap 1B 8
Greenfern Av. SL1: Slou 5F 9
Greenfields SL6: Maid 6H 7
Green La. SL1: Burn 2F 9 & 6A 4
SL2: Farn C 5D 4
SL3: Dat 7G 17
SL4: Wind 1K 21
SL6: Bray, Maid 6H 7
SL6: Fifi 7K 13
TW18: Staines 7K 25
TW20: Egh 3H 25
(Avenue, The)
TW20: Egh 4H 25
(Vicarage Dr.)
TW20: Thorpe 7J 25
Green La. Ct. SL1: Burn 2F 9
Green Leys SL6: Maid 2G 7
Greenock Rd. SL1: Slou 5K 9
Green Pk. TW18: Staines 2K 25
Greenside SL2: Slou 4K 9
Greenway SL1: Burn 1E 8
Greenway, The SL1: Slou 7G 9
Greenways TW20: Egh 4E 24
Greenways Dr. SL6: Maid 4B 6
Gregory Dr. SL4: Old Win 5G 23
Gregory Rd. SL2: Hedg 1F 5
Grenfell SL6: Maid 4J 7
Grenfell Av. SL6: Maid 6G 7
Grenfell Pl. SL6: Maid 6G 7
Grenfell Rd. SL6: Maid 5F 7
(not continuous)
Grenville Cl. SL1: Burn 1E 8
Gresham Rd. SL1: Slou 5K 9
Greystoke Rd. SL2: Slou 4J 9
Griffin Cl. SL1: Slou 1B 16
SL6: Maid 7F 7
Gringer Hill SL6: Maid 3E 6
Grosvenor Ct. SL1: Slou 5D 10
Grosvenor Dr. SL6: Maid 4J 7
Grove, The SL1: Slou 1F 17
TW20: Egh 4G 25
Grove Cl. SL1: Slou 2F 17
SL4: Old Win 6G 23
Grove Ct. TW20: Egh 4G 25
Grove Rd. SL1: Burn 2G 9
SL4: Wind 1B 22
SL6: Maid 5G 7
(not continuous)
Guards Club Rd. SL6: Maid 5K 7
Guards Rd. SL4: Wind 1F 21
Guards Wlk. SL4: Wind 1F 21
Gullet Path SL6: Maid 7E 6
Gwendale SL6: Maid 3D 6
Gwent Cl. SL6: Maid 1C 12
Gwynne Cl. SL4: Wind 7H 15
Gypsy La. SL2: Stoke P 3G 5

H

Haddon Rd. SL6: Maid 7D 6
Hadley Ct. *SL3: Poyle 7F 19*
(off Coleridge Cres.)
Hadlow Ct. SL1: Slou 7B 10
Hag Hill La. SL6: Tap 5D 8
Hag Hill Ri. SL6: Tap 5D 8
Haig Dr. SL1: Slou 1A 16
Halifax Cl. SL6: Maid 4B 6
Halifax Rd. SL6: Maid 4B 6
Halifax Way SL6: Maid 4B 6
Halkingcroft SL3: L'ly 1H 17
Hall Ct. SL3: Dat 6G 17
Hall Mdw. SL1: Burn 1F 9
Halse Dr. SL2: Farn C 3A 4
Hambleden Wlk. SL6: Maid 1F 7
Hamilton Gdns. SL1: Burn 2E 8
Hamilton Pk. SL6: Maid 6B 6
Hamilton Rd. SL1: Slou 5K 9
Hamilton Way SL2: Farn C 4E 4
HAM ISLAND 3J 23
Ham La. SL4: Old Win 4H 23
(not continuous)
TW20: Eng G 3B 24
Hammond End SL2: Farn C 3D 4
Hampden Cl. SL2: Stoke P 2F 11
Hampden Rd. SL3: L'ly 2A 18
SL6: Maid 4C 6
Hampshire Av. SL1: Slou 4B 10
Hanbury Cl. SL1: Burn 4D 8
Hanley Cl. SL4: Wind 7G 15
Hanover Cl. SL1: Slou 2F 17
SL4: Wind 7J 15
TW20: Eng G 5B 24
Hanover Ga. SL1: Slou 7K 9
Hanover Mead SL6: Bray 2K 13
Hanover Way SL4: Wind 1J 21
Harborough Cl. SL1: Slou 7G 9
Harcourt TW19: Wray 5K 23
Harcourt Cl. SL6: Dor R 2C 14
TW20: Egh 5J 25
Harcourt Rd. SL4: Wind 7H 15
SL6: Dor R 2C 14
Hardell Cl. TW20: Egh 4G 25
Harding Spur SL3: L'ly 5A 18
Hardwick Cl. SL6: Maid 4A 6
Hardy Cl. SL1: Slou 7K 9
Harefield Rd. SL6: Maid 5B 6
Harehatch La. SL1: Burn 1A 4
SL2: Farn C 1A 4
Hare Shoots SL6: Maid 7F 7
Harewood Pl. SL1: Slou 2F 17
Hargrave Rd. SL6: Maid 4E 6
Harkness Rd. SL1: Burn 4E 8
Harmondsworth Moor Waterside 5J 19
Harmondsworth Moor Waterside Vis. Cen. 5J 19
Harrington Cl. SL4: Wind 3J 21
Harris Gdns. SL1: Slou 1B 16
Harrison Way SL1: Slou 7G 9
Harrogate Ct. SL3: L'ly 4B 18
Harrow Cl. SL6: Maid 3F 7
Harrow La. SL6: Maid 3E 6
Harrow Mkt. SL3: L'ly 2B 18
Harrow Rd. SL3: L'ly 2A 18
Hartland Cl. SL1: Slou 7C 10
Hartley Cl. SL3: Stoke P 7K 5
Hartley Copse SL4: Old Win 5F 23
Harvest Hill Rd. SL6: Bray, Maid 1F 13
Harvest Rd. TW20: Eng G 4D 24
Harvey Rd. SL3: L'ly 2C 18
Harwich Rd. SL1: Slou 5K 9
Harwood Gdns. SL4: Old Win 6G 23
Haslemere Rd. SL4: Wind 7K 15
Hasting Cl. SL6: Bray 3K 13
Hastings Mdw. SL2: Stoke P 7H 5
Hatch, The SL4: Wind 6F 15
Hatchgate Gdns. SL1: Burn 2G 9
Hatch La. SL4: Wind 2K 21
Hatfield Cl. SL6: Maid 6D 6
Hatfield Rd. SL1: Slou 1F 17
Hatton Av. SL2: Slou 3C 10
Hatton Ct. SL4: Wind 1B 22
Havelock Cres. SL6: Maid 5C 6
Havelock Rd. SL6: Maid 5C 6
Haverlock Bus. Pk. SL6: Maid 5D 6
Hawker Ct. SL3: L'ly 2B 18
Hawkshill Rd. SL2: Slou 2K 9
Hawthorne Av. SL4: Wink 7E 20
Hawthorne Cres. SL1: Slou 5D 10
Hawthorne Dr. SL4: Wink 7E 20
Hawthorne Rd. TW18: Staines 4J 25
Hawthorne Way
SL4: Wink 7E 20
Hawthorn Gdns. SL6: Maid 7F 7
Hawthorn Hill Rd. SL6: Pal S 7E 12
Hawthorn La. SL2: Farn C 6B 4
Hawthorns, The SL3: Poyle 7G 19
Hawtrey Cl. SL1: Slou 1G 17
Hawtrey Rd. SL4: Wind 1B 22
Haymill Rd. SL1: Slou 3G 9
SL2: Slou 3G 9
Haynes Cl. SL3: L'ly 4A 18
Hayse Hill SL4: Wind 7G 15
Haywards Mead SL4: Eton W 4J 15
Hazel Cl. TW20: Eng G 5B 24
Hazelhurst Rd. SL1: Burn 1F 9
Hazell Cl. SL6: Maid 4G 7
Hazell Way SL2: Stoke P 6H 5
Hazlemere Rd. SL2: Slou 7G 11
Headington Cl. SL6: Maid 5B 6
Headington Pl. *SL2: Slou 7E 10*
(off Mill St.)
Headington Rd. SL6: Maid 4B 6
Hearne Dr. SL6: Holy 4H 13
Heathacre SL3: Coln 7F 19
Heathcote SL6: Bray 3J 13
Heathcote Ct. *SL4: Wind 2C 22*
(off Osbourne Rd.)
Heatherside Gdns. SL2: Farn C 2F 5
Heathlands Dr. SL6: Maid 6B 6
Heathrow Cl. UB7: Lford 7J 19
HEDGERLEY 1F 5
HEDGERLEY HILL 1F 5
Hedgerley Hill SL2: Hedg 2F 5
Hedingham M. SL6: Maid 5E 6
Helena Rd. SL4: Wind 1C 22
Helston La. SL4: Wind 7A 16
Helvellyn Cl. TW20: Egh 6H 25
Hemming Way SL2: Slou 2A 10
Hempson Av. SL3: L'ly 2H 17
Hemsdale SL6: Maid 3C 6
Hemwood Rd. SL4: Wind 2G 21
Hencroft St. Nth. SL1: Slou 1E 16
Hencroft St. Sth. SL1: Slou 2E 16
Hendons Way SL6: Holy 4J 13
Henley Rd. SL1: Slou 5H 9
SL6: Maid 5A 6
Henry Rd. SL1: Slou 1C 16
Heritage Ct. *TW20: Egh 4G 25*
(off Station Rd.)
Hermitage Cl. SL3: L'ly 2H 17
Hermitage La. SL4: Wind 2K 21
Herndon Cl. TW20: Egh 3G 25
Heron Dr. SL3: L'ly 3C 18
Heronfield TW20: Eng G 5C 24
HRH PRINCESS CHRISTIAN'S HOSPITAL 7B 16
Herschel Pk. Dr. SL1: Slou 1E 16
Herschel St. SL1: Slou 1E 16
Hetherington Cl. SL2: Slou 2J 9
Hever Cl. SL6: Maid 6D 6
Heynes Grn. SL6: Maid 2C 12
Heywood Av. SL6: Maid 4B 12
Heywood Ct. SL6: Maid 4B 12
Heywood Ct. Cl. SL6: Maid 3B 12
Heywood Gdns. SL6: Maid 3B 12
Hibbert Rd. SL6: Bray 2H 13
Hibbert's All. SL4: Wind 7C 16
Highfield Cl. TW20: Eng G 5C 24
Highfield Ct. SL2: Farn R 7D 4
Highfield La. SL6: Maid 1B 12
Highfield Rd. SL4: Wind 2J 21
SL6: Maid 4C 6
TW20: Eng G 5C 24
Highgrove Pk. SL6: Maid 4F 7
Highlands SL2: Farn C 4E 4
High St. SL1: Burn 2F 9
SL1: Slou 2B 16
(Chalvey)
SL1: Slou 1E 16
(Slough, not continuous)
SL3: Coln 6D 18
SL3: Dat 7G 17
SL3: L'ly 4A 18
SL4: Eton 5C 16
SL4: Wind 7C 16
SL6: Bray 1K 13
SL6: Maid 5G 7
(not continuous)
SL6: Tap 3B 8
TW19: Wray 5K 23
TW20: Egh 4F 25
High St. W. SL1: Slou 1D 16
High Town Rd. SL6: Maid 6F 7
(not continuous)
HIGHWAY 6C 6
Highway Av. SL6: Maid 5B 6
Highway Rd. SL6: Maid 6C 6
Hillary Rd. SL3: L'ly 1K 17
Hillersdon SL2: Slou 4G 11
Hill Farm Rd. SL6: Tap 1B 8
Hillmead Ct. SL6: Tap 4C 8
Hill Pl. SL2: Farn C 6D 4
Hillrise SL3: L'ly 5B 18
Hillside SL1: Slou 1D 16
SL6: Maid 7E 6
Hillview Rd. TW19: Wray 5J 23
Hilperton Rd. SL1: Slou 1D 16
Hindhay La. SL6: Maid 1C 6
Hinksey Cl. SL3: L'ly 2C 18
Hinton Rd. SL1: Slou 6H 9
Hitcham La. SL1: Burn 2B 8
SL6: Burn, Tap 2B 8
Hitcham Rd. SL1: Burn 4D 8
SL6: Tap 5C 8
Hobbis Dr. SL6: Maid 6B 6
HOCKLEY HOLE 7K 5
Hockley La. SL2: Stoke P 6K 5
Hogarth Cl. SL1: Slou 6H 9
Hogfair La. SL1: Burn 2F 9
Holbrook Ct. TW20: Egh 4J 25
Holbrook Mdw. TW20: Egh 5J 25
Hollow Hill La. SL0: Iver 1D 18
Hollybush Hill SL2: Stoke P 6J 5
Holly Cl. SL2: Farn C 3E 4
TW20: Eng G 5B 24
Hollycombe TW20: Eng G 3C 24
Holly Cres. SL4: Wind 1G 21

Holly Dr. SL4: Old Win . . . 4D 22
SL6: Maid . . . 4G 7
Holmanleaze SL6: Maid . . . 4H 7
Holmedale SL2: Slou . . . 6H 11
Holmes Place Health and Fitness Club . . . 1F 17
Holmlea Rd. SL3: Dat . . . 7J 17
Holmlea Wlk. SL3: Dat . . . 7H 17
Holmwood Cl. SL6: Maid . . . 7C 6
HOLYPORT . . . 5J 13
Holyport Rd. SL6: Holy . . . 5H 13
Holyport St. SL6: Holy . . . 5H 13
Home Farm Way SL3: Stoke P . . . 7K 5
Home Mdw. SL2: Farn R . . . 1B 10
Homers Rd. SL4: Wind . . . 7G 15
Homestead Rd. SL6: Maid . . . 1E 12
Homewood SL3: G Grn . . . 5J 11
Hornbeam Gdns. SL1: Slou . . . 2F 17
Horseguards Dr. SL6: Maid . . . 5J 7
Horsemoor Cl. SL3: L'ly . . . 3B 18
Horsham Reach SL6: Maid . . . 2K 7
Horton Cl. SL6: Maid . . . 3K 7
Horton Gdns. SL3: Hort . . . 2K 23
Horton Grange SL6: Maid . . . 3K 7
Horton Rd. SL3: Coln, Hort . . . 7B 18
SL3: Dat, Hort . . . 6G 17
Household Cavalry Mus. . . . 2B 22
Howard Av. SL2: Slou . . . 4C 10
Howarth Rd. SL6: Maid . . . 6H 7
Hoylake Cl. SL1: Slou . . . 1H 15
Hubert Rd. SL3: L'ly . . . 2J 17
Hudson Pl. SL3: L'ly . . . 4A 18
Hughenden Cl. SL6: Maid . . . 6D 6
Hughenden Rd. SL1: Slou . . . 5C 10
Hull Cl. SL1: Slou . . . 1B 16
Humber Way SL3: L'ly . . . 3B 18
Hummer Rd. TW20: Egh . . . 3G 25
Hungerford Av. SL2: Slou . . . 4D 10
Hungerford Dr. SL6: Maid . . . 1F 7
Hunstanton Cl. SL3: Coln . . . 6D 18
Huntercombe Cl. SL6: Tap . . . 5E 8
Huntercombe La. Nth. SL1: Slou . . . 4F 9
Huntercombe La. Sth. SL6: Tap . . . 7E 8
Hunter Ct. SL1: Slou . . . 4F 9
Hunters M. SL4: Wind . . . 7B 16
Hunters Way SL1: Slou . . . 7H 9
Huntingfield Way TW20: Egh . . . 6K 25
Hunts La. SL6: Tap . . . 1B 8
Hurricane Way SL3: L'ly . . . 4C 18
Hurstfield Dr. SL6: Tap . . . 5E 8
Hurst Rd. SL1: Slou . . . 4G 9
Hurworth Av. SL3: L'ly . . . 2H 17
Huxtable Gdns. SL6: Bray . . . 4A 14
Hyde, The SL6: Maid . . . 4G 7
Hylle Cl. SL4: Wind . . . 7H 15
HYTHE END . . . 1H 25
Hythe End Rd. TW19: Wray . . . 1F 25
Hythe Fld. Av. TW20: Egh . . . 5K 25
Hythe Pk. Rd. TW20: Egh . . . 4J 25
Hythe Rd. TW18: Staines . . . 4K 25

I

Ibbotson Ct. SL3: Poyle . . . 7F 19
Ilchester Cl. SL6: Maid . . . 7D 6
Ilex Cl. TW20: Eng G . . . 6B 24
Illingworth SL4: Wind . . . 2H 21
Imperial Ct. SL4: Wind . . . 2K 21
Imperial Rd. SL4: Wind . . . 2K 21
India Rd. SL1: Slou . . . 1G 17
Ingleglen SL2: Farn C . . . 4D 4
Ingleside SL3: Poyle . . . 7F 19
Inkerman Rd. SL4: Eton W . . . 3J 15
Institute Rd. SL6: Tap . . . 5C 8
In-the-Ray SL6: Maid . . . 4J 7
Iona Cres. SL1: Slou . . . 5H 9
Ipswich Rd. SL1: Slou . . . 5J 9
Island, The TW19: Wray . . . 2G 25
UB7: Lford . . . 6K 19
Island Cl. TW18: Staines . . . 3K 25
Islet Pk. SL6: Maid . . . 1K 7
Islet Pk. Dr. SL6: Maid . . . 1K 7
Islet Rd. SL6: Maid . . . 1J 7
Ismay Ct. SL2: Slou . . . 5D 10
Iver Station (Rail) . . . 1G 19
Ives Rd. SL3: L'ly . . . 2A 18
Ivy Cl. SL6: Holy . . . 6H 13
Ivy Cres. SL1: Slou . . . 6J 9

J

Jacob Cl. SL4: Wind . . . 7H 15
Jakes Ho. SL6: Maid . . . 4H 7
James Mdw. SL3: L'ly . . . 5A 18
James St. SL4: Wind . . . 7C 16
Jarratt Ho. *SL4: Wind* . . . *2A 22*
(off St Leonard's Rd.)
Jefferson Cl. SL3: L'ly . . . 3B 18
Jellicoe Cl. SL1: Slou . . . 1A 16
Jennery La. SL1: Burn . . . 2F 9
Jesus Hospital SL6: Bray . . . 2K 13
John F Kennedy Memorial . . . 1C 24
John Taylor Ct. SL1: Slou . . . 7B 10
Jones Way SL2: Hedg . . . 1F 5
Jourdelays Pas. SL4: Eton . . . 5C 16
Journeys End SL2: Stoke P . . . 4D 10
Jubilee Arch SL4: Wind . . . 7C 16
Jubilee Way SL3: Dat . . . 6H 17
Judy's Pas. SL4: Eton . . . 4B 16
Juniper Ct. SL1: Slou . . . 1F 17
Juniper Dr. SL6: Maid . . . 4J 7
Jutland Ho. SL4: Wind . . . 1J 21
Jutland Pl. TW20: Egh . . . 4J 25

K

Kaywood Cl. SL3: L'ly . . . 2J 17
Keates La. SL4: Eton . . . 5B 16
Keble Rd. SL6: Maid . . . 4E 6
Keel Dr. SL1: Slou . . . 1A 16
Keeler Cl. SL4: Wind . . . 2H 21
Keepers Farm Cl. SL4: Wind . . . 1H 21
(not continuous)
Kelpatrick Rd. SL1: Slou . . . 5G 9
Kelsey Cl. SL6: Maid . . . 2E 12
Kempe Cl. SL3: L'ly . . . 3D 18
Kemsley Chase SL2: Farn R . . . 7E 4
Kendal Cl. SL2: Slou . . . 6F 11
Kendal Dr. SL2: Slou . . . 6F 11
Kendall Pl. SL6: Maid . . . 1D 12
Kendrick Rd. SL3: Slou . . . 2G 17
Kenilworth Cl. SL1: Slou . . . 2E 16
Kenneally SL4: Wind . . . 1F 21
Kenneally Cl. SL4: Wind . . . 1F 21
Kenneally Pl. SL4: Wind . . . 1F 21
Kenneally Row *SL4: Wind* . . . *1F 21*
(off Liddell Sq.)
Kenneally Wlk. *SL4: Wind* . . . *1F 21*
(off Guards Rd.)
Kennedy Cl. SL2: Farn C . . . 5E 4
SL6: Maid . . . 6D 6
Kennedy Ho. *SL1: Slou* . . . *7G 9*
(off Harrison Way)
Kennet Rd. SL6: Maid . . . 4G 7
Kennett Rd. SL3: L'ly . . . 2C 18
Kent Av. SL1: Slou . . . 4B 10
Kentons La. SL4: Wind . . . 1H 21
Kent Way SL6: Maid . . . 3F 7
Kenwood Cl. SL6: Maid . . . 5B 6
Keppel Spur SL4: Old Win . . . 6G 23
Kepple St. SL4: Wind . . . 1C 22
Kestrel Path SL2: Slou . . . 3H 9
Keswick Ct. SL2: Slou . . . 6E 10
Keswick Rd. TW20: Egh . . . 6H 25
Kidderminster Rd. SL2: Slou . . . 2K 9
Kidwells Cl. SL6: Maid . . . 5G 7
Kidwells Pk. Dr. SL6: Maid . . . 5G 7
Killarney Dr. SL6: Maid . . . 5F 7
Kiln La. SL2: Hedg . . . 1E 4
Kiln Pl. SL6: Maid . . . 1B 6
Kimber Cl. SL4: Wind . . . 2K 21
Kimberley Cl. SL3: L'ly . . . 3A 18
Kimbers Dr. SL1: Burn . . . 2G 9
Kimbers La. SL6: Maid . . . 2F 13
Kinburn Dr. TW20: Egh . . . 4E 24
King Acre Ct. TW18: Staines . . . 2K 25
King Edward VII Av. SL4: Wind . . . 6D 16
KING EDWARD VII HOSPITAL . . . 2B 22
King Edward Ct. SL4: Wind . . . 7C 16
King Edward Ct. Shop. Cen. SL4: Wind . . . 7B 16
King Edward St. SL1: Slou . . . 1C 16
Kingfisher Ct. SL2: Slou . . . 3A 10
Kinghorn La. SL6: Maid . . . 1E 6
Kinghorn Pk. SL6: Maid . . . 1E 6
King John La. TW19: Wray . . . 4J 23
King John's Cl. TW19: Wray . . . 4J 23
Kingsbury Cres. TW18: Staines . . . 3K 25
Kingsbury Dr. SL4: Old Win . . . 6F 23
Kings Dr. SL6: Maid . . . 6F 7
Kingsfield SL4: Wind . . . 7G 15
Kings Gro. SL6: Maid . . . 6F 7
Kings Gro. Ind. Est. SL6: Maid . . . 6F 7
Kings La. TW20: Eng G . . . 4A 24
Kingsley Av. TW20: Eng G . . . 5B 24
Kingsley Path SL2: Slou . . . 3G 9
Kingsmead Ho. SL1: Slou . . . 7B 10
Kings Rd. SL1: Slou . . . 2D 16
SL4: Wind . . . 3C 22
TW20: Egh . . . 3G 25
Kingstable St. SL4: Eton . . . 6C 16
Kings Ter. SL3: L'ly . . . 5C 18
King St. SL6: Maid . . . 5G 7
(not continuous)
Kingsway SL2: Farn C . . . 5D 4
Kingswood Cl. TW20: Eng G . . . 3D 24
Kingswood Ct. SL6: Bray . . . 7G 7
Kingswood Creek TW19: Wray . . . 4J 23
Kingswood Ho. SL2: Slou . . . 4B 10
Kingswood Ri. TW20: Eng G . . . 4D 24
Kinnaird Cl. SL1: Tap . . . 5F 9
Kipling Ct. SL4: Wind . . . 1A 22
Kirkwall Spur SL1: Slou . . . 4D 10
Knightsbridge Ct. *SL3: L'ly* . . . *3B 18*
(off High St.)
Knights Cl. SL4: Wind . . . 7G 15
TW20: Egh . . . 5K 25
Knights Pl. SL4: Wind . . . 2B 22
Knolton Way SL2: Slou . . . 5G 11
Knowsley Cl. SL6: Maid . . . 3B 6
Kola Ct. SL2: Slou . . . 5G 11
Kotan Dr. TW18: Staines . . . 3J 25

L

Laburnham Rd. SL6: Maid . . . 6E 6
Laburnum Gro. SL3: L'ly . . . 5C 18
Laburnum Pl. TW20: Eng G . . . 5B 24
Lacey Cl. TW20: Egh . . . 6K 25
Ladbrooke Rd. SL1: Slou . . . 2B 16
Lady Astor Ct. SL1: Slou . . . 1D 16
Ladyday Pl. SL1: Slou . . . 7B 10
Laggan Rd. SL6: Maid . . . 2G 7
Laggan Sq. SL6: Maid . . . 3G 7
Lake Av. SL1: Slou . . . 6C 10
LAKE END . . . 1E 14
Lake End Ct. SL6: Tap . . . 5D 8
Lake End Rd. SL4: Dor . . . 2E 14
SL6: Dor R, Tap . . . 6E 8
Lakeside SL6: Maid . . . 2J 7
Lakeside Dr. SL2: Stoke P . . . 7G 5
Lakeside Ind. Est. SL3: Coln . . . 5G 19
Lakeside Rd. SL0: Rich P . . . 6G 19
SL3: Coln, Rich P . . . 6G 19
Lake Vw. SL6: Maid . . . 3H 7
Lake Vw. Cvn. Site SL4: Wink . . . 7B 20
Lambert Av. SL3: L'ly . . . 2K 17
Lambourne Dr. SL6: Maid . . . 2D 12
Lambton Ho. SL4: Wind . . . 2K 21
Lammas Av. SL4: Wind . . . 1B 22
Lammas Cl. TW18: Staines . . . 2K 25
Lammas Ct. SL4: Wind . . . 1B 22
TW19: Staines . . . 1K 25
Lammas Dr. TW18: Staines . . . 3K 25
Lammas Rd. SL1: Slou . . . 4G 9
Lancaster Av. SL2: Slou . . . 3B 10
Lancaster Cl. TW20: Eng G . . . 4D 24
Lancaster Rd. SL6: Maid . . . 4C 6
Lancastria M. SL6: Maid . . . 5E 6
Lancelot Cl. SL1: Slou . . . 1K 15
Langdale Cl. SL6: Maid . . . 6H 7
Langham Pl. TW20: Egh . . . 4F 25
LANGLEY . . . 2B 18
Langley Broom SL3: L'ly . . . 4A 18
Langley Bus. Cen. SL3: L'ly . . . 1B 18
Langley Bus. Pk. SL3: L'ly . . . 1B 18
Langley Hall . . . *2B 18*
(off Langley Rd.)
Langley Leisure Cen. . . . 3C 18
Langley Pk. Country Pk. . . . 4K 11
Langley Pk. Rd. SL3: L'ly . . . 1B 18
Langley Quay SL3: L'ly . . . 1B 18
Langley Rd. SL3: L'ly . . . 1H 17
LANGLEY RDBT. . . . 5B 18
Langley Station (Rail) . . . 1B 18
Langleywood Sports & Playcentre . . . 2K 17
Langton Cl. SL1: Slou . . . 7G 9
SL6: Maid . . . 3E 6
Langton's Mdw. SL2: Farn C . . . 5E 4
Langton Way TW20: Egh . . . 5J 25
Langworthy End SL6: Holy . . . 5J 13
Langworthy La. SL6: Holy . . . 5H 13
Lansdowne Av. SL1: Slou . . . 7D 10
Lansdowne Ct. SL1: Slou . . . 7D 10
Lantern Wlk. SL6: Maid . . . 5J 7
Larch Cl. SL2: Slou . . . 4A 10
Larchfield Rd. SL6: Maid . . . 7E 6
Larchmoor Pk. SL2: Stoke P . . . 4J 5
Larchwood Dr. TW20: Eng G . . . 5B 24
Larkings La. SL2: Stoke P . . . 7K 5
Larksfield TW20: Eng G . . . 6B 24
La Roche Cl. SL3: L'ly . . . 2H 17
Lascelles Rd. SL3: Slou . . . 2G 17
Lassell Ct. SL6: Maid . . . 5J 7
Lassell Gdns. SL6: Maid . . . 5J 7
Laurel Av. SL3: L'ly . . . 1K 17
TW20: Eng G . . . 4B 24
Laurel Cl. SL3: Poyle . . . 6F 19
Lawkland SL2: Farn R . . . 2B 10
Lawn Av. UB7: W Dray . . . 1K 19
Lawn Cl. SL3: Dat . . . 6H 17
Lawns, The SL3: Poyle . . . 7F 19

Lawrence Ct. SL4: Wind 1B 22
Lawrence Way SL1: Slou 4F 9
Laxton Grn. SL6: Maid 2D 12
Layburn Cres. SL3: L'ly 5C 18
Lea, The TW20: Egh 6J 25
Leaholme Gdns. SL1: Slou 4F 9
Ledger La. SL6: Fifi 1A 20
Ledgers Rd. SL1: Slou 1C 16
Leeds Rd. SL1: Slou 6D 10
Lee La. SL6: Maid 1A 6
Lees Cl. SL6: Maid 7C 6
Lees Gdns. SL6: Maid 7C 6
Leeson Gdns.
SL4: Eton W 3H 15
Legoland 4G 21
Leigh Pk. SL3: Dat 6G 17
Leigh Rd. SL1: Slou 6A 10
Leigh Sq. SL4: Wind 1G 21
Leighton Gdns. SL6: Maid 3J 7
Leiston Spur SL1: Slou 5D 10
Leith Cl. SL1: Slou 7F 11
LENT 3E 8
Lent Grn. SL1: Burn 3E 8
(not continuous)
Lent Grn. La. SL1: Burn 3E 8
LENT RISE 4E 8
Lent Ri. Rd. SL1: Burn 5E 8
SL6: Tap 5E 8
Lerwick Dr. SL1: Slou 4D 10
Leslie Dunne Ho. SL4: Wind 1H 21
Lewes Ct. SL1: Slou 1B 16
Lewins Farm Ct. SL1: Slou 6J 9
Lewins Way SL1: Slou 6J 9
Leworth Pl. SL4: Wind 7C 16
Lexington Av. SL6: Maid 7E 6
Liddell SL4: Wind 2F 21
Liddell Pl. SL4: Wind 1F 21
Liddell Sq. SL4: Wind 1F 21
Liddell Way SL4: Wind 2F 21
Lidstone Ct. SL3: G Grn 5J 11
Lilac Ct. SL2: Slou 2J 9
Lilley Way SL1: Slou 7H 9
Lillibrooke Cres. SL6: Maid 2B 12
Lily Dr. UB7: W Dray 3K 19
Lime Av. SL4: Wind 7E 16
Limes, The SL4: Wind 1F 21
Limes M. TW20: Egh 4F 25
Limes Rd. TW20: Egh 4F 25
Lime Wlk. SL6: Maid 4B 6
Linchfield Rd. SL3: Dat 7H 17
Lincoln Ct. SL1: Slou 2D 16
Lincoln Hatch La. SL1: Burn 3F 9
Lincoln Rd. SL6: Maid 4C 6
Lincoln Way SL1: Slou 6G 9
Linden SL3: L'ly 4C 18
Linden Av. SL6: Maid 3E 6
Linden Ct. TW20: Eng G 5B 24
Linden Dr. SL2: Farn R 7E 4
Lindores Rd. SL6: Holy 5J 13
Lingfield Cvn. Pk. SL6: Bray 5A 14
Lingholm Cl. SL6: Maid 6D 6
Link, The SL2: Slou 5G 11
Link Rd. SL3: Dat 7H 17
Linkswood Rd. SL1: Burn 1F 9
Lismore Pk. SL2: Slou 5E 10
Lissett Rd. SL6: Maid 6H 7
Litcham Spur SL1: Slou 5C 10
Littlebrook Av. SL2: Slou 3H 9
Little Buntings SL4: Wind 2J 21
Lit. Chapels Way SL1: Slou 1K 15
Littlecroft Rd. TW20: Egh 4F 25
Littledown Rd. SL1: Slou 7E 10
LITTLEFIELD GREEN 7A 12
Littlefield Grn. SL6: W Walt 7A 12
Littleport Spur SL1: Slou 5D 10
Lit. Sutton La. SL3: L'ly 4D 18
Little Woodlands SL4: Wind 2J 21
LITTLEWORTH COMMON 2A 4
Littleworth Rd. SL1: Burn 1A 4
Liverpool Rd. SL1: Slou 5A 10
Lochinvar Cl. SL1: Slou 1A 16
Lock Av. SL6: Maid 2K 7
Lockbridge Ct. SL6: Maid 4J 7
Locke Gdns. SL3: L'ly 1H 17
Lockets Cl. SL4: Wind 7G 15
Lock La. SL6: Maid 1D 12
Lock Mead SL6: Maid 2K 7
Lock Path SL4: Dor, Eton W 5G 15
Loddon Dr. SL6: Maid 4E 6
Loddon Spur SL1: Slou 6D 10
Lodge Cl. SL1: Slou 1B 16
TW20: Eng G 4D 24
Lodge Way SL4: Wind 2H 21
London Rd. GU25: Vir W 7B 24
SL3: Dat 6G 17
(not continuous)
SL3: L'ly 2H 17
TW20: Eng G 7B 24
Longbourn SL4: Wind 2K 21
Long Cl. SL2: Farn C 6D 4
Long Dr. SL1: Burn 2F 9
Longfield SL2: Hedg 2F 5
LONGFORD 7J 19
Longford Cir. UB7: Lford 7J 19
LONGFORDMOOR 7H 19
Long Furlong Dr. SL2: Slou 3G 9
Long La. SL6: Holy, Pal S 7F 13
(not continuous)
Longleat Gdns. SL6: Maid 6E 6
Longmead SL4: Wind 7H 15
Long Readings La. SL2: Slou 2A 10
Longside Cl. TW20: Egh 7J 25
Long Wlk., The SL4: Wind 7C 22
Longwood Av. SL3: L'ly 4C 18
Longworth Dr. SL6: Maid 3K 7
Lonsdale Cl. SL6: Maid 3H 7
Lonsdale Way SL6: Holy 4K 13
Look Ahead SL1: Slou 1D 16
Loosen Dr. SL6: Maid 2B 12
Lord Mayor's Dr. SL2: Farn C 5B 4
(not continuous)
Lord Raglan Ho. SL4: Wind 2B 22
Loring Rd. SL4: Wind 7J 15
Lorne Cl. SL1: Slou 2A 16
Lorne Ct. SL1: Slou 2B 16
Losfield Rd. SL4: Wind 7H 15
Lotus Pk. TW18: Staines 3K 25
Lovegrove Dr. SL2: Slou 3J 9
Lovejoy La. SL4: Wind 1G 21
Lovett Gdns. SL6: Maid 1J 7
Lovett Rd. TW18: Staines 3H 25
Lowbrook Dr. SL6: Maid 2B 12
Lwr. Boyndon Rd. SL6: Maid 6F 7
Lwr. Britwell Rd. SL2: Slou 3G 9
(not continuous)
Lwr. Cippenham La. SL1: Slou 7H 9
Lwr. Cookham Rd. SL6: Maid 1K 7
Lwr. Lees Rd. SL2: Slou 2K 9
Lowestoft Dr. SL1: Slou 5G 9
Luddington Av. GU25: Vir W 7F 25
Ludlow Rd. SL6: Maid 6F 7
Luff Cl. SL4: Wind 2H 21
Lundy Ct. SL1: Slou 6H 9
Lutman La. SL6: Maid 2G 7
Lydford Av. SL2: Slou 4C 10
Lydsey Cl. SL2: Slou 2K 9
Lyell Pl. E. SL4: Wind 2F 21
Lyell Pl. W. SL4: Wind 2F 21
Lyell Rd. SL4: Wind 2F 21
Lyell Wlk. E. SL4: Wind 2F 21
Lyell Wlk. W. SL4: Wind 2F 21
LYNCH HILL 2H 9
Lynch Hill La. SL2: Slou 3H 9
Lynden Cl. SL6: Holy 5J 13
Lyndwood Dr. SL4: Old Win 5F 23
Lyndwood Pde. *SL4: Old Win 5F 23*
(off St Luke's Rd.)
Lyneham Gdns. SL6: Maid 3C 6
Lynton Grn. SL6: Maid 5F 7
Lynwood Av. SL3: L'ly 2J 17
TW20: Egh 5E 24
Lysander Mead SL6: Maid 4K 7

M

McAuliffe Dr. SL2: Farn C 3B 4
Mackenzie Mall *SL1: Slou 1E 16*
(off Wellington St.)
Mackenzie St. SL1: Slou 1E 16
Madeira Wlk. SL4: Wind 7C 16
Mafeking Rd. TW19: Wray 1H 25
Magna Carta La. TW19: Wray 7J 23
Magna Carta Monument 1D 24
Magna Rd. TW20: Eng G 5B 24
Magnet Leisure Cen. 5H 7
Magnolia Gdns. SL3: L'ly 2H 17
Magpie Way SL2: Slou 3J 9
MAIDENHEAD 5G 7
Maidenhead Bri. SL6: Maid 5K 7
Maidenhead Bus. Campus, The
SL6: Lit G 3A 12
MAIDENHEAD COURT 1K 7
Maidenhead Ct. Pk. SL6: Maid 1J 7
MAIDENHEAD HUNTERCOMBE HOSPITAL 6F 9
Maidenhead Rd. SL4: Wind 6F 15
SL6: Maid 2F 7
Maidenhead Station (Rail) 6G 7
Maidenhead United FC 6H 7
Main Dr. SL0: Rich P 3F 19
Main Rd. SL4: Wind 6F 15
Majors Farm Rd. SL3: Dat 6J 17
Malders La. SL6: Maid 1B 6
Malet Cl. TW20: Egh 5K 25
Mallard Cl. SL1: Burn 1E 8
Mallard Dr. SL1: Slou 6J 9
Mallow Pk. SL6: Maid 3D 6
Malpas Rd. SL2: Slou 6G 11
Malt Hill TW20: Egh 4E 24
Malt Ho. Cl. SL4: Old Win 6G 23
Maltings, The TW18: Staines 3K 25
Malton Av. SL1: Slou 5A 10
Malvern Ct. SL3: L'ly 5B 18
Malvern Rd. SL6: Maid 3E 6
Mandeville Ct. TW20: Egh 3G 25
Manfield Cl. SL2: Slou 2K 9
Manor Ct. SL1: Slou 7J 9
Manorcrofts Rd. TW20: Egh 5G 25
Mnr. Farm Cl. SL4: Wind 2J 21
Mnr. Farm Cotts. SL4: Old Win 4F 23
Mnr. Farm Ct. TW20: Egh 4G 25
MANOR FARM ESTATE 6H 23
Mnr. Farm Ho. SL4: Wind 2J 21
Mnr. Farm La. TW20: Egh 4G 25
Manor Gro. SL6: Fifi 7A 14
Manor Ho. La. SL3: Dat 6G 17
Manor La. SL6: Maid 1F 13
Manor Leaze TW20: Egh 4H 25
MANOR PARK 4C 10
Manor Pk. TW18: Staines 2K 25
Manor Rd. SL4: Wind 1H 21
SL6: Maid 1F 13
Manor Way SL6: Holy 5H 13
TW20: Egh 5F 25
Mansel Cl. SL2: Slou 4G 11
Mansell Cl. SL4: Wind 7H 15
Mansion Cvn. Site SL0: Iver 1D 18
Mansion La. SL0: Iver 1D 18
Maple Cl. SL6: Maid 7D 6
Maple Ct. SL4: Wind 2B 22
TW20: Eng G 5B 24
Maple Cres. SL2: Slou 6G 11
Mapledurham Wlk. SL6: Maid 1F 7
Maplin Pk. SL3: L'ly 1C 18
Marbeck Cl. SL4: Wind 7G 15
Marcia Ct. SL1: Slou 7J 9
Marescroft Rd. SL2: Slou 3H 9
Marina Way SL1: Slou 6G 9
Marish Ct. SL3: L'ly 2B 18
Marish Wharf SL3: L'ly 1K 17
Market La. SL3: L'ly 2D 18
Market Pl. SL3: Coln 6D 18
Market St. SL4: Wind 7C 16
SL6: Maid 5G 7
Marlborough Cl. SL6: Maid 6B 6
Marlborough Rd. SL3: L'ly 3J 17
SL6: Maid 6B 6
Marlow Rd. SL6: Maid 5G 7
(Bailey Cl.)
SL6: Maid 1A 6
(Lee La.)
Marshfield SL3: Dat 7H 17
Marsh La. SL4: Dor 1C 14
SL6: Dor, Dor R, Tap 7B 8
Martin Cl. SL4: Wind 7F 15
Martin Rd. SL1: Slou 2D 16
SL6: Maid 4G 7
Martin's Plain SL2: Stoke P 2E 10
Marunden Grn. SL2: Slou 2J 9
Mary Drew Almshouses TW20: Eng G 5D 24
Mary Morgan Ct. SL2: Slou 4C 10
Maryside SL3: L'ly 1K 17
Mascoll Path SL2: Slou 2J 9
Masons Ct. SL1: Slou 6H 9
Masons Rd. SL1: Slou 6H 9
Mathisen Way SL3: Poyle 7F 19
Maybury Cl. SL1: Slou 5G 9
Mayfield Cvn. Pk. UB7: W Dray 2K 19
Mayfield Dr. SL4: Wind 2K 21
Mayflower Way SL2: Farn C 4E 4
Maynard Ct. SL4: Wind 7K 15
Maypole Rd. SL6: Tap 4D 8
Mead Av. SL3: L'ly 1C 18
Mead Cl. SL3: L'ly 1C 18
TW20: Egh 5H 25
Mead Ct. TW20: Egh 5J 25
Meadfield Av. SL3: L'ly 1B 18
Meadfield Rd. SL3: L'ly 2B 18
Meadowbank SL6: Maid 7B 6
Mdw. Brook Cl. SL3: Poyle 7G 19
Meadow Cl. SL4: Old Win 4G 23
Meadow Ct. TW18: Staines 2K 25
Meadow Gdns. TW18: Staines 4K 25
Meadow La. SL4: Eton W 5A 16
Meadow Rd. SL3: L'ly 2K 17
Meadow Vw. La. SL6: Holy 5F 13
Meadow Way SL4: Old Win 5G 23
SL6: Dor R 1C 14
SL6: Fifi 7A 14
Meads, The SL4: Wind 1K 21
Mead Wlk. SL3: L'ly 1C 18
Mead Way SL1: Slou 4G 9
SL6: Maid 5G 7
Medallion Pl. SL6: Maid 5J 7

Mede Cl. TW19: Wray .7J 23
Mede Ct. TW18: Staines .2K 25
Medlake Pl. TW20: Egh .6J 25
Medlake Rd. TW20: Egh .5J 25
Medlar Ct. SL2: Slou .7H 11
Megabowl
Maidenhead .4G 7
Melbourne Av. SL1: Slou .5B 10
Mellor Wlk. *SL4: Wind .7C 16*
(off Batchelors Acre)
Melton Ct. *SL6: Maid .6G 7*
(off Cullerns Pas.)
Mendip Cl. SL3: L'ly .4B 18
Mercian Way SL1: Slou .7G 9
Mercia Rd. SL6: Maid .1C 12
Mere Rd. SL1: Slou .2E 16
Merlin Cl. SL3: L'ly .5C 18
Merlin Ct. SL6: Maid .4C 6
Merton Cl. SL6: Maid .2D 12
Merton Rd. SL1: Slou .2F 17
Merwin Way SL4: Wind .1G 21
Meryton Ho. SL4: Wind .2K 21
Michael Cl. SL6: Maid .7D 6
Midcroft SL2: Slou .3A 10
MIDDLE GREEN .7K 11
Middle Grn. SL3: L'ly .7K 11
Middlegreen Rd. SL3: L'ly .1J 17
Middlegreen Trad. Est.
SL3: L'ly .1J 17
Middle Hill TW20: Egh, Eng G .3C 24
Middle Wlk. SL1: Burn .2E 8
Mildenhall Rd. SL1: Slou .5D 10
Milford Ct. SL1: Slou .1F 17
Millbrook Way SL3: Poyle .7F 19
Mill Cl. UB7: W Dray .2K 19
Mill Ct. SL2: Slou .7E 10
Millers Ct. TW20: Egh .5K 25
Miller's La. SL4: Old Win .5E 22
Mill La. SL4: Wind .6K 15
SL6: Tap .5K 7
Mill Pl. SL3: Dat .1J 23
Mill Pl. Cvn. Pk. SL3: Dat .1H 23
Mill Rd. UB7: W Dray .2K 19
Millside Ct. SL0: Thorn .1J 19
Millside Pk. SL4: Wink .7C 20
Mills Spur SL4: Old Win .6G 23
Millstream La. SL1: Slou .7H 9
Mill St. SL2: Slou .7E 10
SL3: Coln .6E 18
Mill West SL2: Slou .7E 10
Milner Rd. SL1: Burn .4D 8
Milton Rd. SL2: Slou .3C 10
TW20: Egh .4F 25
Milverton Cl. SL6: Maid .2C 12
Mina Av. SL3: L'ly .1J 17
Minniecroft Rd. SL1: Burn .2E 8
Minster Way SL3: L'ly .1A 18
Minton Ri. SL6: Tap .5E 8
Mirador Cres. SL2: Slou .6G 11
Misbourne Ct. SL3: L'ly .3B 18
Missenden Gdns. SL1: Burn .5E 8
Mitchell Cl. SL1: Slou .1K 15
Moat Dr. SL2: Slou .4H 11
Moffy Hill SL6: Maid .2F 7
Molyns M. SL1: Slou .7H 9
Money La. UB7: W Dray .2K 19
MONEYROW GREEN .6H 13
Moneyrow Grn. SL6: Holy .7G 13
Monkey Island La. SL6: Bray .2A 14
Monksfield Way SL2: Slou .3K 9
Monks Rd. SL4: Wind .1G 21
Mons Wlk. TW20: Egh .4J 25
Montague Rd. SL1: Slou .6E 10
Montagu Rd. SL3: Dat .7G 17
Montem La. SL1: Slou .7C 10
Montem Sports Cen. .1C 16
Montgomery Pl. SL2: Slou .5H 11
Montpelier Ct. SL4: Wind .1B 22
Montrose Av. SL1: Slou .5A 10
(not continuous)
SL3: Dat .6H 17
Montrose Dr. SL6: Maid .6B 6
Montrose Way SL3: Dat .7J 17
Monycrower Dr. SL6: Maid .5F 7
MOOR, THE .1K 25
Moorbridge Rd. SL6: Maid .5H 7
Moore Cl. SL1: Slou .1A 16
Moore Gro. Cres.
TW20: Egh .5F 25
Moor End SL6: Holy .4K 13
Moores La. SL4: Eton W .3J 15
Moorfield Ter. SL6: Maid .4H 7
Moor Furlong SL1: Slou .7H 9
Moorings, The SL4: Wind .6F 15
MOOR JUNC. .6J 19
Moorland Rd. UB7: Harm .5K 19
Moorlands Dr. SL6: Maid .4A 6
Moor La. SL6: Maid .3G 7
Moor La. TW18: Staines .2K 25
TW19: Staines .1K 25
(not continuous)
UB7: Harm .5K 19
Moorside Cl. SL6: Maid .3G 7
Moorstown Ct. SL1: Slou .1D 16
Moray Dr. SL2: Slou .5F 11
Moreau Wlk. SL3: G Grn .5K 11
Moreland Av. SL3: Coln .6D 18
Moreland Cl. SL3: Coln .6D 18
Morello Dr. SL3: L'ly .1A 18
Moreton Way SL1: Slou .7G 9
Morley Cl. SL3: L'ly .1A 18
Morrice Cl. SL3: L'ly .3A 18
Mortimer Rd. SL3: L'ly .2J 17
Morton Dr. SL2: Farn C .4A 4
Mossy Va. SL6: Maid .3E 6
Moundsfield Way SL1: Slou .1H 15
Mountbatten Cl. SL1: Slou .2F 17
Mountbatten Sq. SL4: Wind .7B 16
Mount Cl. SL2: Farn C .3E 4
Mt. Hill La. SL9: Ger X .1K 5
Mount Lee TW20: Egh .4F 25
Mounts Hill SL4: Wink .7F 21
Mowbray Cres. TW20: Egh .4G 25
Muddy La. SL2: Slou .4D 10
Mulberry Av. SL4: Wind .2E 22
Mulberry Dr. SL3: L'ly .4K 17
Mulberry Wlk. SL6: Maid .4D 6
Mullens Rd. TW20: Egh .4H 25
Mundesley Spur SL1: Slou .5D 10
Mundy Ct. SL4: Eton .5C 16
Murrin Rd. SL6: Maid .4D 6
Mus. of Eton Life .5C 16
Myers Dr. SL2: Farn C .4D 4
MYRKE .3E 16
Myrke, The SL3: Dat .3E 16
Myrtle Cl. SL3: Poyle .7F 19
Myrtle Cres. SL2: Slou .6E 10

N

Napier Rd. SL6: Maid .6C 6
Nash Rd. SL3: L'ly .3A 18
NHS WALK-IN CENTRE (SLOUGH) *2E 16*
(in Upton Hospital)
Needham Cl. SL4: Wind .7H 15
Nelson Cl. SL3: L'ly .3J 17
Nelson Rd. SL4: Wind .2J 21
Neptune Way SL1: Slou .1H 15
Neville Cl. SL2: Stoke P .5H 5
Neville Ct. SL1: Burn .2F 9
Newbeach Ho. SL2: Slou .2A 10
Newberry Cres. SL4: Wind .1G 21
Newbery Way SL1: Slou .1C 16
Newbury Dr. SL6: Maid .6J 7
Newchurch Rd. SL2: Slou .4J 9
New Cut SL1: Burn .3D 8
Newhaven Spur SL2: Slou .3A 10
Newlands Dr. SL6: Maid .5B 6
Newnham Cl. SL2: Slou .7E 10
Newport Rd. SL2: Slou .3H 9
New Rd. SL3: Dat .7J 17
SL3: L'ly .2B 18
SL6: Holy .5J 13
TW18: Staines .4J 25
New Sq. SL1: Slou .1D 16
New Sta. Ho. SL2: Slou .7E 10
Newton Cl. SL3: L'ly .1A 18
Newton Ct. SL4: Old Win .5F 23
Newton La. SL4: Old Win .5G 23
Newtonside Orchard SL4: Old Win .5F 23
New Wickham La. TW20: Egh .6G 25
NEW WINDSOR .2C 22
Nicholas Gdns. SL1: Slou .7H 9
Nicholls SL4: Wind .2F 21
Nicholls Wlk. SL4: Wind .2F 21
Nicholson M. *TW20: Egh .4G 25*
(off Nicholson Wlk.)
Nicholsons La. SL6: Maid .5G 7
Nicholsons Wlk. SL6: Maid .5G 7
Nicholson Wlk. TW20: Egh .4G 25
Nightingale Ct. SL1: Slou .2F 17
Nightingale La. SL6: Maid .1E 6
Nightingale Pk. SL2: Farn C .6B 4
Nightingale Shott TW20: Egh .5F 25
Nightingale Wlk. SL4: Wind .2B 22
Nine Acres SL1: Slou .7J 9
Nixey Cl. SL1: Slou .1F 17
Noble Ct. *SL2: Slou .7E 10*
(off Mill St.)
Nobles Way TW20: Egh .5E 24
Norden Cl. SL6: Maid .1D 12
Norden Farm Cen. for the Arts .7D 6
Norden Mdws. SL6: Maid .7D 6
Norden Rd. SL6: Maid .7D 6
Norelands Dr. SL1: Burn .1F 9
Norfolk Av. SL1: Slou .4B 10
Norfolk Pk. Cotts. SL6: Maid .4G 7
Norfolk Rd. SL6: Maid .4F 7
Normandy Wlk. TW20: Egh .4J 25
Normans, The SL2: Slou .5G 11
Norreys Dr. SL6: Maid .1D 12
Northampton Av. SL1: Slou .5B 10
Northborough Rd. SL2: Slou .3K 9
Nth. Burnham Cl. SL1: Burn .1E 8
North Cl. SL4: Wind .7J 15
Northcroft SL2: Slou .3A 10
Northcroft Cl. TW20: Eng G .4B 24
Northcroft Gdns. TW20: Eng G .4B 24
Northcroft Rd. TW20: Eng G .4B 24
Northcroft Vs. TW20: Eng G .4B 24
North Dean SL6: Maid .3G 7
North Dr. SL2: Stoke P .2D 10
Northern Rd. SL2: Slou .3C 10
Northfield Rd. SL4: Eton W .3J 15
SL6: Maid .3G 7
North Grn. SL1: Slou .6D 10
SL6: Maid .3G 7
Northmead Rd. SL2: Slou .3J 9
North Pk. SL0: Rich P .2D 18
North Rd. SL6: Maid .5F 7
Nth. Star La. SL6: Maid .6D 6
North St. SL4: Wink .7E 20
TW20: Egh .4F 25
North Ter. SL4: Wind .6C 16
NORTH TOWN .3G 7
Nth. Town Cl. SL6: Maid .3G 7
Nth. Town Mead SL6: Maid .3G 7
Nth. Town Moor SL6: Maid .2G 7
Nth. Town Rd. SL6: Maid .3G 7
Northumbria Rd. SL6: Maid .1C 12
Norway Dr. SL2: Slou .4G 11
Notley End TW20: Eng G .6C 24
Nursery La. SL3: L'ly .7J 11
Nursery Pl. SL4: Old Win .5G 23
Nursery Rd. SL6: Tap .5E 8
Nursery Way TW19: Wray .5J 23

O

Oak Av. TW20: Egh .6J 25
Oaken Gro. SL6: Maid .4C 6
Oakfield Av. SL1: Slou .7A 10
Oakhurst SL6: Maid .1J 7
Oak La. SL4: Wind .7K 15
TW20: Eng G .2C 24
Oakley Ct. SL4: Wat O .5D 14
Oakley Cres. SL1: Slou .6D 10
OAKLEY GREEN .1E 20
Oakley Grn. Rd. SL4: Oak G, Wat O .1B 20
(not continuous)
Oakridge Pl. SL2: Farn C .3E 4
Oak Stubbs La. SL6: Dor R .1C 14
Oak Tree Dr. TW20: Eng G .4C 24
Oaktree Dr. SL3: L'ly .4C 18
Oast Ho. Cl. TW19: Wray .6K 23
Oatlands Dr. SL1: Slou .5C 10
Oban Ct. SL1: Slou .1C 16
Observatory Shop. Cen., The
SL1: Slou .1F 17
Ockwells Rd. SL6: Maid .2C 12
Odencroft Rd. SL2: Slou .2K 9
Oldacres SL6: Maid .5J 7
Old Beaconsfield Rd. SL2: Farn C .5E 4
Old Ct. Cl. SL6: Maid .2C 12
Old Courtyard, The TW20: Egh .5F 25
Old Crown SL1: Slou .1E 16
Oldershaw M. SL6: Maid .4C 6
Old Ferry Dr. TW19: Wray .5H 23
Oldfield Rd. SL6: Maid .6J 7
Old Fives Ct. SL1: Burn .2E 8
Old Forge Cl. SL6: Bray .2H 13
Old Ho. Ct. SL3: Wex .4J 11
Old Marsh La. SL6: Tap .1C 14
Old Mill La. SL6: Bray .1K 13
Old Nursery Ct. SL2: Hedg .1E 4
Old School Ct. TW19: Wray .6K 23
Old School M. TW18: Staines .4K 25
Old Slade La. SL0: Rich P .2F 19
Oldway La. SL1: Slou .6F 9
(not continuous)
OLD WINDSOR .5F 23
Old Windsor Lock SL4: Old Win .4H 23
Olivia Dr. SL3: L'ly .4A 18
Omega Way TW20: Thorpe .7J 25
One Pin La. SL2: Farn C .3E 4
Opal Ct. SL3: Wex .3H 11
Opeck's Cl. SL2: Stoke P .3G 11
Opendale Rd. SL1: Burn .4E 8
Orchard Av. SL1: Slou .4G 9
SL4: Wind .7K 15
Orchard Cl. SL6: Bray .2H 13
TW20: Egh .4H 25

Orchard Ct. UB7: Lford 6K **19**
Orchard Ga. SL2: Farn C 4E **4**
Orchard Gro. SL6: Maid 5D **6**
Orchard Rd. SL4: Old Win 5G **23**
Orchards Res. Pk. SL3: L'ly 7K **11**
Orchardville SL1: Burn 3E **8**
Orchard Way SL3: L'ly 7K **11**
Orchid Ct. TW20: Egh 3H **25**
Orwell Cl. SL4: Wind 2C **22**
Osborne Ct. SL4: Wind 1B **22**
Osborne M. SL4: Wind 1B **22**
Osborne Rd. SL4: Wind 1B **22**
TW20: Egh 5F **25**
Osborne St. SL1: Slou 1E **16**
Osier Pl. TW20: Egh 5J **25**
Osney Rd. SL6: Maid 2F **7**
Ostler Ga. SL6: Maid 3D **6**
Ouseley Lodge *SL4: Old Win 6H 23*
(off Ouseley Rd.)
Ouseley Rd. SL4: Old Win 6H **23**
(not continuous)
TW19: Wray 6H **23**
Owen Cl. SL3: L'ly 4A **18**
Oxford Av. SL1: Burn 1E **8**
SL1: Slou 4J **9**
Oxford Rd. SL4: Wind 7B **16**
Oxford Rd. E. SL4: Wind 7B **16**

P

Padbury Oaks UB7: Lford 7J **19**
Paddock, The SL3: Dat 7G **17**
SL4: Wink 7E **20**
SL6: Maid 2D **6**
Paddock Cl. SL6: Maid 3B **12**
Padstow Cl. SL3: L'ly 1K **17**
Paget Dr. SL6: Maid 1B **12**
Paget Rd. SL3: L'ly 3A **18**
Pagoda, The SL6: Maid 3J **7**
Palace Cl. SL1: Slou 7J **9**
PALEY STREET 7C **12**
Paley St. SL6: Pal S 7C **12**
Palmers Cl. SL6: Maid 2B **12**
Palmerston Av. SL3: Slou 2G **17**
Pamela Row SL6: Holy 5H **13**
Pantile Row SL3: L'ly 3B **18**
Parade, The SL4: Wind 7G **15**
TW18: Staines 4K **25**
Parish La. SL2: Farn C 1D **4**
Park & Ride
Windsor (Home Park) 5D **16**
Windsor (Legoland) 4H **21**
Park Av. TW19: Wray 4J **23**
TW20: Egh 5J **25**
Park Cl. SL4: Wind 1C **22**
Park Cnr. SL4: Wind 2H **21**
Parkgate SL1: Burn 3F **9**
Parkland Av. SL3: L'ly 3J **17**
Park La. SL1: Burn 1A **4**
SL3: Slou 2G **17**
SL4: Wink 7E **20**
Park Lawn SL2: Farn R 2B **10**
Park Ride SL4: Wind 6G **21**
Park Rd. SL2: Farn R, Stoke P 1B **10**
TW20: Egh 3G **25**
Parkside SL6: Maid 3E **6**
Parkside Lodge *SL3: Slou 2F 17*
(off Upton Ct. Rd.)
Parkside Wlk. SL1: Slou 2F **17**
Park Sq. SL4: Wink 7E **20**
Park St. SL1: Slou 2E **16**
(not continuous)
SL3: Coln 7E **18**
SL4: Wind 7C **16**
SL6: Maid 5G **7**
Parkview Chase SL1: Slou 5H **9**
Parlaunt Rd. SL3: L'ly 3B **18**
Parry Grn. Nth. SL3: L'ly 3A **18**
Parry Grn. Sth. SL3: L'ly 3B **18**
Parsonage La. SL2: Farn C, Farn R 5E **4**
SL4: Wind 7K **15**
Parsonage Rd. TW20: Eng G 4D **24**
Parsons Rd. SL3: L'ly 4A **18**
Parson's Wood La. SL2: Farn C 6F **5**
Partridge Mead SL6: Maid 2G **7**
Patricia Cl. SL1: Slou 6H **9**
Paul Ct. TW20: Egh 4K **25**
Paxton Av. SL1: Slou 2B **16**
Pearce Cl. SL6: Maid 3G **7**
Pearce Rd. SL6: Maid 3G **7**
Pearl Gdns. SL1: Slou 7A **10**
Peartree Cl. SL1: Slou 7J **9**
Peascod Pl. *SL4: Wind 7C 16*
(off Peascod St.)
Peascod St. SL4: Wind 7B **16**
Peel Cl. SL4: Wind 2A **22**
Peel Ct. SL1: Slou 4A **10**
Pegasus Ct. TW20: Egh 4H **25**
Pelham Ct. SL6: Maid 5F **7**
Pelling Hill SL4: Old Win 6G **23**
Pemberley Lodge SL4: Wind 2K **21**
Pemberton Rd. SL2: Slou 3H **9**
Pendeen Ct. SL1: Slou 7K **9**
Penn Ho. SL1: Burn 2F **9**
Pennine Rd. SL2: Slou 4K **9**
Penn Mdw. SL2: Stoke P 7H **5**
Penn Rd. SL2: Slou 3C **10**
SL3: Dat 7J **17**
Pennylets Grn.
SL2: Stoke P 6H **5**
Penrose Ct. TW20: Eng G 5D **24**
(not continuous)
Penshurst Rd. SL6: Maid 7E **6**
Pentland Rd. SL2: Slou 4K **9**
Penwood Ct. SL6: Maid 5C **6**
Penyston Rd. SL6: Maid 6D **6**
Penzance Spur SL2: Slou 3A **10**
Pepler Way SL1: Burn 2E **8**
Pepys Cl. SL3: L'ly 5C **18**
Percy Pl. SL3: Dat 7G **17**
Perrycroft SL4: Wind 2H **21**
Perryfields Way SL1: Burn 3E **8**
Perry Ho. SL1: Burn 3E **8**
Perryman Way SL2: Slou 2J **9**
Perth Av. SL1: Slou 5A **10**
Perth Trad. Est. SL1: Slou 4A **10**
Peterhead M. SL3: L'ly 4B **18**
Petersfield Av. SL2: Slou 7F **11**
Peters La. SL6: Holy 5J **13**
Petty Cross SL1: Slou 5H **9**
Petworth Ct. SL4: Wind 7K **15**
Pevensey Rd. SL2: Slou 4K **9**
Pheasants Cft. SL6: Maid 1B **12**
Philbye M. SL1: Slou 1J **15**
Phipps Cl. SL6: Maid 3B **12**
Phipps Rd. SL1: Slou 4G **9**
(not continuous)
Phoenix Ct. SL6: Maid 1E **12**
Pickford Dr. SL3: L'ly 7K **11**
Pickfords Gdns. SL1: Slou 7D **10**
Pierson Rd. SL4: Wind 7G **15**
Pine Cl. SL6: Maid 5C **6**
Piner Cotts. SL4: Wind 2H **21**
Pines, The SL3: L'ly 7K **11**
Pine Trees Bus. Pk. TW18: Staines 4K **25**
Pine Way TW20: Eng G 5B **24**
Pink La. SL1: Burn 1E **8**
Pinkneys Dr. SL6: Maid 5A **6**
PINKNEYS GREEN 3A **6**
Pinkneys Rd. SL6: Maid 4B **6**
Pinnacle Leisure Cen. 1G **11**
Pipers Cl. SL1: Burn 2F **9**
Pitts Rd. SL1: Slou 7B **10**
Plackett Way SL1: Slou 7G **9**
Plaines Cl. SL1: Slou 7J **9**
Plain Ride SL4: Wind 7F **21**
Plough La. SL2: Stoke P 7K **5**
Plough Lees La. SL1: Slou 6D **10**
Pluto Cl. SL1: Slou 1H **15**
Plymouth Rd. SL1: Slou 4H **9**
Pococks La. SL4: Eton 4D **16**
Points, The SL6: Maid 2C **12**
Pollard Cl. SL4: Old Win 4G **23**
Pond Rd. TW20: Egh 5J **25**
Pooley Av. TW20: Egh 4H **25**
POOLEY GREEN 4J **25**
Pooley Grn. Cl. TW20: Egh 4J **25**
Pooley Grn. Rd. TW20: Egh 4H **25**
Pool La. SL1: Slou 6D **10**
Poolmans Rd. SL4: Wind 2G **21**
Popes Cl. SL3: Coln 6C **18**
Poplar Cl. SL3: Poyle 7F **19**
Poplar Ho. SL3: L'ly 4A **18**
Poplars Gro. SL6: Maid 2J **7**
Portland Bus. Cen. *SL3: Dat 7G 17*
(off Manor Ho. La.)
Portland Cl. SL2: Slou 3G **9**
Portlock Rd. SL6: Maid 5D **6**
Portsmouth Ct. SL1: Slou 6D **10**
Post Office La. SL3: G Grn 5J **11**
Poulcott TW19: Wray 5K **23**
Pound, The SL1: Burn 3G **9**
Powerleague Soccer Cen.
Chalvey 2C **16**
Powis Cl. SL6: Maid 1C **12**
Powney Rd. SL6: Maid 5D **6**
POYLE 7F **19**
Poyle La. SL1: Burn 1E **8**
Poyle New Cotts. SL3: Poyle 7G **19**
Poyle Rd. SL3: Poyle 7F **19**
Poynings, The SL0: Rich P 3G **19**
Precinct, The TW20: Egh 4G **25**
Precincts, The SL1: Burn 3E **8**
Preston Rd. SL2: Slou 6H **11**
Prestwood SL2: Slou 5G **11**
Priest Hill SL4: Old Win 2C **24**
TW20: Eng G, Old Win 2C **24**
Primrose Dr. UB7: W Dray 3K **19**
Primrose La. SL6: Holy 7H **13**
Prince Albert's Wlk. SL4: Wind 7F **17**
Prince Andrew Cl. SL6: Maid 4J **7**
Prince Andrew Rd. SL6: Maid 3J **7**
Prince Consort Cotts. SL4: Wind 1C **22**
Prince Consort's Dr. SL4: Wind 5J **21**
(not continuous)
Princes Cl. SL4: Eton W 4J **15**
Princes Rd. TW20: Egh 5F **25**
Princess Av. SL4: Wind 2A **22**
PRINCESS MARGARET BMI HOSPITAL 1C **22**
Princess St. SL6: Maid 6G **7**
Princes St. SL1: Slou 1G **17**
Priors Cl. SL1: Slou 2F **17**
SL6: Bray 3J **13**
Priors Rd. SL4: Wind 2G **21**
Priors Way SL6: Bray 3J **13**
Priors Way Ind. Est. SL6: Bray 3J **13**
Priory Ct. TW20: Egh 5J **25**
Priory Rd. SL1: Slou 4F **9**
Priory Way SL3: Dat 6G **17**
Progress Bus. Cen. SL1: Slou 5G **9**
Prospect La. TW20: Eng G 4A **24**
Prospect Pl. *SL4: Wind 2C 22*
(off Osbourne Rd.)
Providence Pl. SL6: Maid 5G **7**
Prune Hill TW20: Egh, Eng G 6D **24**
Pumpkin Hill SL1: Burn 5A **4**
Pursers Ct. SL2: Slou 5D **10**
Purssell Cl. SL6: Maid 2B **12**
Purton Ct. SL2: Farn R 6E **4**
Purton La. SL2: Farn C, Farn R 6E **4**

Q

Quantock Cl. SL3: L'ly 4B **18**
Quaves Rd. SL3: Slou 2G **17**
Queen Adelaide's Ride SL4: Wink 5G **21**
Queen Anne's Rd. SL4: Wind 3B **22**
(not continuous)
Queen Ann's Ct. *SL4: Wind 7C 16*
(off Peascod St.)
Queen Charlotte St. *SL4: Wind 7C 16*
(off High St.)
QUEEN ELIZABETH HOUSE 4C **24**
Queen Elizabeth's Wlk. SL4: Wind 1D **22**
Queens Acre SL4: Wind 3C **22**
Queens Acre Ho. SL4: Wind 2C **22**
Queen's Cl. SL4: Old Win 4F **23**
Queens Ct. SL1: Slou 6E **10**
Queens Ga. Cotts. SL4: Wind 3C **22**
Queensmead SL3: Dat 6G **17**
Queensmere Rd. SL1: Slou 1E **16**
Queensmere Shop. Cen. SL1: Slou 1E **16**
Queens Rd. SL1: Slou 6E **10**
SL3: Dat 6G **17**
SL4: Eton W 4J **15**
SL4: Wind 1B **22**
TW20: Egh 4F **25**
Queens Ter. SL4: Wind 2C **22**
Queen St. SL6: Maid 6G **7**
(not continuous)
Queensway SL6: Maid 3F **7**
Queen Victoria Wlk. SL4: Wind 7D **16**
Quelmans Head Ride SL4: Wind 7G **21**
Quinbrookes SL2: Slou 5H **11**
Quincy Rd. TW20: Egh 4G **25**

R

Radcot Av. SL3: L'ly 2C **18**
Radcot Cl. SL6: Maid 1F **7**
Radnor Way SL3: L'ly 3K **17**
Ragstone Rd. SL1: Slou 2D **16**
Railway Ter. SL2: Slou 7E **10**
TW18: Staines 4K **25**
Rainsborough Chase SL6: Maid 2C **12**
Raleigh Cl. SL1: Slou 7K **9**
Ralston Ct. *SL4: Wind 7C 16*
(off Russell St.)
Rambler Cl. SL6: Tap 5E **8**
Rambler La. SL3: L'ly 2H **17**
Ramsey Ct. SL2: Slou 3G **9**
Randall Cl. SL3: L'ly 4A **18**
Randall Ct. *SL4: Old Win 5F 23*
(off Lyndwood Dr.)
Randolph Rd. SL3: L'ly 2K **17**
Ranelagh SL4: Wink 7E **20**
Ravenfield TW20: Eng G 5C **24**
Ravens Fld. SL3: L'ly 1J **17**
Ravensworth Rd. SL2: Slou 2K **9**
Ray Dr. SL6: Maid 5J **7**
Ray Lea Cl. SL6: Maid 4J **7**

Ray Lea Rd. SL6: Maid .3J 7
Ray Lodge M. SL6: Maid .5J 7
Ray Mead Ct. SL6: Maid .3K 7
Ray Mdw. SL6: Maid .3H 7
Ray Mead Rd. SL6: Maid .5K 7
Ray Mill Rd. E. SL6: Maid .3H 7
Ray Mill Rd. W. SL6: Maid .4G 7
Raymond Cl. SL3: Poyle .7F 19
Raymond Rd. SL3: L'ly .2B 18
SL6: Maid .5E 6
Rayners Cl. SL3: Coln .6D 18
Ray Pk. Av. SL6: Maid .3J 7
Ray Pk. La. SL6: Maid .5J 7
Ray Pk. Rd. SL6: Maid .4J 7
Ray's Av. SL4: Wind .6J 15
Ray St. SL6: Maid .5J 7
Rectory Cl. SL2: Farn R .2B 10
SL4: Wind .7K 15
Rectory Rd. SL6: Tap .3A 8
Red Cott. M. SL3: L'ly .2H 17
Red Ct. SL1: Slou .7D 10
Reddington Dr. SL3: L'ly .3K 17
Redford Rd. SL4: Wind .7G 15
Redriff Cl. SL6: Maid .6E 6
Redwood SL1: Burn .1E 8
Redwood Gdns. SL1: Slou .6C 10
Redwoods, The SL4: Wind .2C 22
Reeve Rd. SL6: Holy .5J 13
Reform Rd. SL6: Maid .5J 7
Regal Ct. SL6: Bray .3J 13
Regent Ct. SL1: Slou .5D 10
SL4: Wind .7C 16
SL6: Maid .5G 7
Reid Av. SL6: Maid .7E 6
Repton Cl. SL6: Maid .2D 12
Retreat, The SL6: Fifi .6A 14
TW20: Eng G .4D 24
Revesby Cl. SL6: Maid .2E 12
Rhodes Cl. TW20: Egh .4H 25
Rhodes Ct. *TW20: Egh .4J 25*
(off Pooley Grn. Cl.)
Ribstone Rd. SL6: Maid .2C 12
Ricardo Rd. SL4: Old Win .5G 23
Richards Way SL1: Slou .7H 9
RICHINGS PARK .1G 19
Richings Pl. SL0: Rich P .2F 19
Richings Way SL0: Rich P .2F 19
Richmond Cres. SL1: Slou .7F 11
Rickman's La. SL2: Stoke P .5G 5
Ridgebank SL1: Slou .6J 9
Ridge Ct. SL4: Wind .2B 22
Ridgemead Rd. TW20: Eng G .2A 24
Riding Ct. Farm SL3: Dat .5G 17
Riding Ct. Rd. SL3: Dat, L'ly .6H 17
Ridings, The SL0: Rich P .3G 19
SL4: Wind .6F 15
SL6: Maid .6B 6
Rigby Lodge SL1: Slou .5D 10
Ripley Av. TW20: Egh .5E 24
Ripley Cl. SL3: L'ly .3K 17
RIPLEY SPRINGS .5E 24
Risborough Rd. SL6: Maid .4F 7
Riseley Rd. SL6: Maid .5E 6
Riverbank, The SL4: Wind .6A 16
River Ct. SL6: Tap .5K 7
River Gdns. SL6: Bray .1A 14
River Pk. Av. TW18: Staines .3K 25
River Rd. SL4: Wind .6F 15
SL6: Tap .6K 7
Riverside TW19: Wray .6H 23
TW20: Egh .2G 25
Riverside Pk. SL3: Poyle .7F 19
Riverside Wlk. *SL4: Wind .6C 16*
(off Thames Side)
River St. SL4: Wind .6C 16
Rixman Cl. SL6: Maid .7E 6
Rixon Cl. SL3: G Grn .5K 11
Roasthill La. SL4: Dor .5G 15
Robert Rd. SL2: Hedg .1F 5
Roberts Way TW20: Eng G .6C 24
Robin Hood Cl. SL1: Slou .7J 9
Robin Pde. SL2: Farn C .4E 4
Robin Willis Way SL4: Old Win .5F 23
Rochester Rd. TW18: Staines .5K 25
Rochfords Gdns. SL2: Slou .6H 11
Rochford Way SL6: Tap .6D 8
Rockall Ct. SL3: L'ly .2C 18
Rodney Way SL3: Poyle .7F 19
Roebuck Grn. SL1: Slou .7H 9
Rogers La. SL2: Stoke P .6H 5
Rokesby Rd. SL2: Slou .2J 9
Rolls La. SL6: Holy .5F 13
Romney Lock SL4: Wind .5D 16
Romney Lock Rd. SL4: Wind .6C 16
Romney Wlk. SL4: Wind .6C 16
Romsey Cl. SL3: L'ly .2A 18
Romsey Dr. SL2: Farn C .2F 5
Ronaldsay Spur SL1: Slou .4D 10
Rosehill Ct. SL1: Slou .2F 17
Roseleigh Cl. SL6: Maid .5B 6
Roses La. SL4: Wind .1G 21
Rose Wlk. SL2: Slou .4A 10
Rosewood Way SL2: Farn C .4E 4
Rosken Gro. SL2: Farn R .1A 10
Rossiter Cl. SL3: L'ly .3K 17
Ross Rd. SL6: Maid .7E 6
Roundway TW20: Egh .4J 25
Rowan Av. TW20: Egh .4J 25
Rowanhurst Dr. SL2: Farn C .4E 4
Rowan Way SL2: Slou .4A 10
Rowland Cl. SL4: Wind .2G 21
Rowley La. SL3: Wex .1J 11
Roxborough Way SL6: Maid .2A 12
Roxwell Cl. SL1: Slou .7H 9
Royal Free Ct. *SL4: Wind .7C 16*
(off Batchelors Acre)
Royal Holloway
University of London .5D 24
Royal Holloway University Sports Cen. .6E 24
Royal M. SL4: Wind .7C 16
Royal Windsor Racecourse .5H 15
Roydon Ct. TW20: Egh .5K 25
Royston Way SL1: Slou .4G 9
Ruby Cl. SL1: Slou .1K 15
Ruddlesway SL4: Wind .1G 21
(not continuous)
Rudsworth Cl. SL3: Coln .7E 18
Runnemede Rd. TW20: Egh .3F 25
RUNNYMEDE .1D 24
Runnymede Ct. TW20: Egh .3G 25
Runnymede Rdbt. TW20: Egh .3H 25
Ruscombe Gdns. SL3: Dat .6F 17
Rusham Ct. TW20: Egh .5G 25
Rusham Pk. Av. TW20: Egh .5F 25
Rusham Rd. TW20: Egh .5F 25
Rushes, The SL6: Maid .6J 7
Rushington Av. SL6: Maid .7G 7
Rushmere Pl. TW20: Eng G .4E 24
Russell Ct. SL6: Maid .5G 7
Russell St. SL4: Wind .7C 16
Russet Rd. SL6: Maid .2D 12
Rutherford Cl. SL4: Wind .7J 15
Rutland Av. SL1: Slou .4B 10
Rutland Ga. SL6: Maid .6D 6
Rutland Pl. SL6: Maid .6D 6
Rutland Rd. SL6: Maid .6E 6
Rycroft SL4: Wind .2J 21
Rydal Way TW20: Egh .6H 25
Rydings SL4: Wind .2J 21
Rye Cl. SL6: Maid .1B 12
Rye Ct. SL1: Slou .2F 17
Rylstone Cl. SL6: Maid .2D 12
Ryvers End SL3: L'ly .2A 18
Ryvers Rd. SL3: L'ly .2A 18

S

Sadlers M. SL6: Maid .5J 7
Saffron Cl. SL3: Dat .7G 17
St Adrians Cl. SL6: Maid .1C 12
St Alban's Cl. SL4: Wind .7C 16
St Alban's St. SL4: Wind .7C 16
St Andrew's Av. SL4: Wind .1J 21
St Andrew's Cl. SL4: Old Win .5F 23
TW19: Wray .5K 23
St Andrews Cotts. *SL4: Wind .1K 21*
(off Cross Oak)
St Andrews Ct. *SL1: Slou .2D 16*
(off Upton Pk.)
St Andrew's Cres. SL4: Wind .1J 21
St Andrew's Way SL1: Slou .6G 9
St Bernards Rd. SL3: L'ly .2H 17
St Catherines Pl. TW20: Egh .4G 25
St Chads Rd. SL6: Maid .1C 12
St Cloud Way SL6: Maid .5G 7
St Columbus Cl. SL6: Maid .1C 12
St Cuthberts Cl. TW20: Eng G .5D 24
St Davids Cl. SL6: Maid .1B 12
St Davids Dr. TW20: Eng G .6C 24
St Elmo Cl. SL2: Slou .3C 10
St Elmo Cres. SL2: Slou .3C 10
St George's Chapel
Windsor .7C 16
St Georges Cl. SL4: Wind .7H 15
St George's Cres. SL1: Slou .6G 9
St Ives Rd. SL6: Maid .5H 7
St James Pl. SL1: Slou .5F 9
St James Wlk. SL0: Rich P .1F 19
St John's Ct. TW20: Egh .4G 25
St John's Dr. SL4: Wind .1K 21
St Johns Rd. SL2: Slou .6F 11
SL4: Wind .1K 21
St Jude's Cl. TW20: Eng G .4C 24
St Jude's Cotts. TW20: Eng G .4C 24
St Judes Rd. TW20: Eng G .2C 24
St Laurence Way SL1: Slou .2F 17
St Leonard's Av. SL4: Wind .1B 22
St Leonard's Hill SL4: Wind .3G 21
St Leonard's Rd. SL4: Wind .2K 21
SL4: Wink .5F 21
St Leonards Wlk. SL0: Rich P .2G 19
St Luke's Rd. SL4: Old Win .5F 23
SL6: Maid .5G 7
St Margarets Rd. SL6: Maid .5B 6
St Mark's Cres. SL6: Maid .5C 6
ST MARK'S HOSPITAL .5D 6
St Marks Pl. SL4: Wind .1B 22
St Marks Rd. SL4: Wind .1B 22
SL6: Maid .5D 6
St Martin's Rd. UB7: W Dray .2K 19
St Mary's Cl. SL6: Maid .5H 7
St Mary's Rd. SL3: L'ly .7K 11
St Mary's Wlk. SL6: Maid .5G 7
St Michaels Ct. SL2: Slou .3G 9
St Nazaire Cl. TW20: Egh .4J 25
St Patricks Cl. SL6: Maid .1C 12
St Pauls Av. SL2: Slou .6E 10
St Paul's Rd. TW18: Staines .4K 25
St Peter's Cl. SL1: Burn .3E 8
SL4: Old Win .4F 23
St Peters Rd. SL4: Old Win .4F 23
SL6: Maid .2E 6
St Thomas Wlk. SL3: Coln .6E 18
Salisbury Av. SL2: Slou .3B 10
Salters Cl. SL6: Maid .5H 7
Salters Rd. SL6: Maid .5J 7
SALT HILL .7B 10
Salt Hill Av. SL1: Slou .7B 10
Salt Hill Dr. SL1: Slou .7B 10
Salt Hill Mans. SL1: Slou .7B 10
Salt Hill Way SL1: Slou .7B 10
Sampson's Grn. SL2: Slou .2J 9
Sandisplatt Rd. SL6: Maid .6B 6
Sandlers End SL2: Slou .3A 10
Sandown Rd. SL2: Slou .4J 9
Sandringham Ct. SL1: Slou .5G 9
Sandringham Rd. SL6: Maid .2F 7
Sands Farm Dr. SL1: Burn .3F 9
Sandy Mead SL6: Holy .4K 13
Sarsby Dr. TW19: Wray .1G 25
Satis Ho. SL3: Dat .6H 17
Savill M. TW20: Eng G .5D 24
Savoy Ct. SL6: Maid .3G 7
Sawyers Cl. SL4: Wind .6H 15
SL6: Maid .3B 12
Sawyers Cres. SL6: Maid .3B 12
Saxon Cl. SL3: L'ly .1A 18
Saxon Gdns. SL6: Tap .3A 8
Saxon Way SL4: Old Win .5G 23
UB7: Harm .5K 19
Saxon Way Ind. Est. UB7: Harm .5K 19
Scafell Rd. SL2: Slou .3J 9
Scarborough Way SL1: Slou .2A 16
Scholars Wlk. SL3: L'ly .1B 18
School Allotment Ride SL4: Wink .6E 20
School La. SL2: Slou .6E 10
SL2: Stoke P .6K 5
SL6: Maid .3F 7
TW20: Egh .4G 25
School Rd. UB7: Harm .5K 19
School Wlk. SL2: Slou .6G 11
Schroder Ct. TW20: Eng G .4B 24
Scotlands Dr. SL2: Farn C .5D 4
Scott Cl. SL2: Farn C .4E 4
Seacourt Rd. SL3: L'ly .3C 18
Second Cres. SL1: Slou .4B 10
Sefton Cl. SL2: Stoke P .7H 5
Sefton Paddock SL2: Stoke P .6J 5
Sefton Pk. SL2: Stoke P .6J 5
Selim Ct. *SL1: Slou .1G 17*
(off Clifton Rd.)
Selwyn Cl. SL4: Wind .1G 21
Selwyn Pl. SL1: Slou .6J 9
Sermed Ct. SL2: Slou .7H 11
Severn Cres. SL3: L'ly .4C 18
Seymour Cl. SL6: Maid .2C 12
Seymour Ho. SL3: L'ly .1K 17
Seymour Rd. SL1: Slou .1B 16
Shackleton Rd. SL1: Slou .6E 10
Shaftesbury Ct. SL1: Slou .1D 16
Shaggy Calf La. SL2: Slou .6F 11
Sharman Row SL3: L'ly .4A 18
Sharney Av. SL3: L'ly .2C 18
Shaw Ct. SL4: Old Win .4F 23
SHAW FARM .3D 22
Shaw Gdns. SL3: L'ly .4A 18
Sheehy Way SL2: Slou .6G 11
Sheepcote Rd. SL4: Eton W .4K 15
SL4: Wind .1H 21
Sheephouse Rd. SL6: Maid .3J 7
Sheet St. SL4: Wind .1C 22
Sheet St. Rd. SL4: Wind .7J 21
Sheffield Rd. SL1: Slou .5B 10

Shelley Cl. SL3: L'ly 4A 18
Shelton Ct. SL3: L'ly 2H 17
Shenston Ct. *SL4: Wind* *7C 16*
(off James St.)
Shenstone Dr. SL1: Burn 3G 9
Shepherds Ct. SL4: Wind 1H 21
Sherborne Cl. SL3: Poyle 7F 19
Sherbourne Dr. SL4: Wind 3J 21
SL6: Maid 2D 12
Sherbourne Wlk. SL2: Farn C 3E 4
Sheridan Ct. SL1: Slou 6H 9
Sherman Rd. SL1: Slou 4D 10
Sherwood Cl. SL3: L'ly 2K 17
Sherwood Ct. SL3: L'ly 4A 18
Sherwood Dr. SL6: Maid 6B 6
Shifford Cres. SL6: Maid 2F 7
Shirley Av. SL4: Wind 7J 15
Shirley Rd. SL6: Maid 7D 6
Shoppenhangers Rd. SL6: Maid 2C 12
Shop Rd. SL4: Wind 6F 15
Shoreham Ri. SL2: Slou 3G 9
Shortfern SL2: Slou 5H 11
Sidney Rd. SL4: Wind 2F 21
Siebel Ct. TW20: Egh 3H 25
Silco Dr. SL6: Maid 6F 7
Silver Cl. SL6: Maid 7B 6
Silverstone M. SL6: Maid 1D 12
Silvertrees Dr. SL6: Maid 7B 6
Simmons Cl. SL3: L'ly 3B 18
Simons Wlk. TW20: Eng G 6C 24
Simpson Cl. SL6: Maid 4J 7
Simpsons Way SL1: Slou 7C 10
Sinclair Rd. SL4: Wind 2B 22
Sir Henry Peakes Dr. SL2: Farn C 5C 4
Sir Robert M. SL3: L'ly 4B 18
Sir Sydney Camm Ho. SL4: Wind 7A 16
Skerries Ct. SL3: L'ly 3B 18
Sky Bus. Cen. TW20: Thorpe 7J 25
Skydmore Path SL2: Slou 2J 9
Skye Lodge *SL1: Slou* *7D 10*
(off Lansdowne Av.)
Skyport Dr. UB7: Harm 6K 19
SLOUGH 1E 16
Slough Crematorium SL2: Slou 5E 10
Slough Ice Arena 7C 10
Slough Indoor Tennis Cen. 7C 10
Slough Ind. Est. SL1: Slou 4K 9
(not continuous)
Slough Mus. 1F 17
Slough Retail Pk. SL1: Slou 7A 10
Slough Rd. SL1: Slou 3D 16
SL3: Dat 4F 17
SL4: Eton 5C 16
Slough Station (Rail) 7E 10
Slough Supapitch 4G 11
Slough Town FC 4F 11
Slough Trad. Est. SL1: Slou 4J 9
(Banbury Av.)
SL1: Slou 5A 10
(Liverpool Rd., not continuous)
Smithfield Cl. SL6: Maid 2A 12
Smithfield Rd. SL6: Maid 2A 12
Smith's La. SL4: Wind 1H 21
Snape Spur SL1: Slou 5D 10
Snowball Hill SL6: Maid 3B 12
(not continuous)
Snowden Cl. SL4: Wind 3G 21
Somerford Cl. SL6: Maid 4J 7
Somersby Cres. SL6: Maid 2F 13
Somerset Way SL0: Rich P 1G 19
Somerville Rd. SL4: Eton 4B 16
Sophie Gdns. SL3: L'ly 1J 17
Sospel Ct. SL2: Farn R 1B 10
South Av. TW20: Egh 5J 25
South Cl. SL1: Slou 6G 9
Southcroft SL2: Slou 3A 10
TW20: Eng G 4B 24
Southfield Cl. SL4: Dor 2F 15
Southfield Gdns. SL1: Burn 4E 8
Southgate Ho. SL6: Maid 5G 7
South Grn. SL1: Slou 6D 10
SOUTHLEA 1G 23
Southlea Rd. SL3: Dat 7G 17
SL4: Wind 3F 23
South Mdw. La. SL4: Eton 5B 16
South Path SL4: Wind 7B 16
South Rd. SL6: Maid 6F 7
TW20: Eng G 5C 24
South Ter. SL4: Wind 7D 16
South Vw. SL4: Eton, Eton W 4A 16
Southwold Spur SL3: L'ly 1D 18
Sovereign Beeches SL2: Farn C 5D 4
Sovereign Hgts. SL3: Dat 5B 18
Spackmans Way SL1: Slou 2B 16
Speedbird Way UB7: Harm 6J 19
Spencer Gdns. TW20: Eng G 4D 24
Spencer Rd. SL3: L'ly 2A 18
Spencers Cl. SL6: Maid 4E 6
Spencers Rd. SL6: Maid 4E 6
Spens SL6: Maid 4G 7
Sperling Rd. SL6: Maid 3G 7
Spinners Wlk. SL4: Wind 7B 16
Spinney SL1: Slou 7A 10
Spinney La. SL4: Wink 7E 20
SPITAL 2A 22
Spitfire Cl. SL3: L'ly 3B 18
Springate Fld. SL3: L'ly 1K 17
Spring Av. TW20: Egh 5E 24
Spring Cl. SL6: Maid 2G 7
Springfield SL1: Slou 2G 17
Springfield Cl. SL4: Wind 1A 22
Springfield Pk. SL6: Holy 4J 13
Springfield Rd. SL3: L'ly 6C 18
SL4: Wind 1A 22
Spring Hill SL6: Maid 2F 13
Spring La. SL1: Slou 7J 9
SL2: Farn R 6D 4
Spring Ri. TW20: Egh 5E 24
Spruce Ct. SL1: Slou 2E 16
Spur, The SL1: Slou 4G 9
Spur Dr. SL1: Slou 4D 10
Square, The UB7: Lford 7J 19
Squirrel Dr. SL4: Wink 7E 20
Squirrel La. SL4: Wink 7E 20
Stafferton Way SL6: Maid 6G 7
Stafford Av. SL2: Slou 3B 10
Stafford Cl. SL6: Tap 5E 8
Stag Meadow 3A 22
Staines Bri. TW18: Staines 4K 25
Staines By-Pass
TW19: Staines 1J 25
Staines Rd. TW19: Wray 6K 23 & 1F 25
Stamford Rd. SL6: Maid 6D 6
Stanhope Rd. SL1: Slou 5G 9
Stanley Cotts. SL2: Slou 7E 10
Stanley Grn. E. SL3: L'ly 3A 18
Stanley Grn. W. SL3: L'ly 3A 18
Stanton Way SL3: L'ly 3K 17
Stanwell Moor Rd. UB7: Lford 7J 19
Starwood Ct. SL3: L'ly 2H 17
Station App. SL6: Maid 6G 7
Station Rd. SL1: Slou 5H 9
SL3: L'ly 2B 18
SL6: Tap 5C 8
TW19: Wray 5K 23
TW20: Egh 4G 25
Station Rd. Nth. TW20: Egh 4G 25
Staunton Rd. SL2: Slou 4C 10
Stephen Cl. TW20: Egh 5J 25
Stephenson Ct. *SL1: Slou* *1E 16*
(off Osborne St.)
Stephenson Dr. SL4: Wind 6A 16
Stevenson Rd. SL2: Hedg 1F 5
Stewart Av. SL1: Slou 4E 10
Stewart Cl. SL6: Fifi 7A 14
Stewart's Dr. SL2: Farn C 3D 4
Stile Rd. SL3: L'ly 2J 17
Stirling Cl. SL4: Wind 1G 21
Stirling Gro. SL6: Maid 4B 6
Stirling Rd. SL1: Slou 4K 9
Stockdales Rd. SL4: Eton W 3J 15
Stockwells SL6: Tap 3A 8
STOKE COMMON 3J 5
Stoke Comn. Rd. SL3: Ful 3J 5
Stoke Ct. Dr. SL2: Stoke P 7G 5
Stoke Gdns. SL1: Slou 7D 10
STOKE GREEN 3G 11
Stoke Grn. SL2: Stoke P 3F 11
Stoke Pk. 6H 5
Stoke Pk. Av. SL2: Farn R 2B 10
STOKE POGES 6J 5
Stoke Poges La. SL1: Slou 7D 10
SL2: Slou, Stoke P 5D 10
Stoke Rd. SL2: Slou, Stoke P 7E 10
Stokesay SL2: Slou 6E 10
Stoke Vw. SL1: Slou 7E 10
Stoke Wood SL2: Stoke P 3H 5
Stompits Rd. SL6: Holy 5J 13
Stomp Rd. SL1: Burn 4E 8
Stonebridge Fld. SL4: Eton 4A 16
Stonefield Pk. SL6: Maid 5D 6
Stoneylands Ct. TW20: Egh 4F 25
Stoneylands Rd. TW20: Egh 4F 25
Stoney La. SL2: Farn R 7C 4
Stoney Meade SL1: Slou 7A 10
Stornaway Rd. SL3: L'ly 3D 18
Stour Cl. SL1: Slou 2A 16
Stovell Rd. SL4: Wind 6A 16
Stowe Rd. SL1: Slou 6H 9
Straight Rd. SL4: Old Win 4F 23
Stranraer Gdns. SL1: Slou 7D 10
Stratfield Ct. SL6: Maid 4J 7
Stratfield Rd. SL1: Slou 1F 17
Stratford Cl. SL2: Slou 3G 9
Stratford Gdns. SL6: Maid 1D 12
Streamside SL1: Slou 7J 9
Strode's Coll. La. *TW20: Egh* *4F 25*
(off High St.)
Strode St. TW20: Egh 3G 25
Stroma Ct. SL1: Slou 6G 9
Stroud Cl. SL4: Wind 2G 21
STROUDE 7G 25
Stroude Rd. TW20: Egh 5G 25
Stroud Farm Rd. SL6: Holy 5J 13
Stuart Cl. SL4: Wind 1J 21
Stuart Way SL4: Wind 1H 21
STUD GREEN 6F 13
Sturt Grn. SL6: Holy 5F 13
Suffolk Cl. SL1: Slou 5H 9
Suffolk Rd. SL6: Maid 1E 12
Sumburgh Way SL1: Slou 4D 10
Summerhouse La. UB7: Harm 5K 19
Summerlea SL1: Slou 7A 10
Summerleaze Rd. SL6: Maid 3H 7
Summers Rd. SL1: Burn 2F 9
Sunbury Ct. SL4: Eton 5C 16
Sunbury Rd. SL4: Eton 5C 16
Sun Cl. SL4: Eton 5C 16
Sunderland Rd. SL6: Maid 4C 6
Sun La. SL6: Maid 5F 7
SUNNYMEADS 3K 23
Sunnymeads Station (Rail) 2K 23
Sun Pas. SL4: Wind 7C 16
Sunray Av. UB7: W Dray 1K 19
Surly Hall Wlk. SL4: Wind 7J 15
Surrey Av. SL2: Slou 4B 10
Sussex Cl. SL1: Slou 1G 17
Sussex Ho. SL2: Farn C 5E 4
Sussex Keep SL1: Slou 1G 17
Sussex Pl. SL1: Slou 1F 17
(not continuous)
Sutherland Grange SL4: Wind 6G 15
SUTTON 4D 18
Sutton Av. SL3: L'ly 1H 17
Sutton Cl. SL6: Maid 6D 6
Sutton La. SL3: L'ly 5C 18
Sutton Pl. SL3: L'ly 5C 18
Swabey Rd. SL3: L'ly 3B 18
Swallowfield TW20: Eng G 5B 24
Swanbrook Ct. SL6: Maid 5H 7
Swann Ct. SL1: Slou 2D 16
Swan Ter. SL4: Wind 6A 16
Sweeps La. TW20: Egh 4F 25
Switchback, The SL6: Maid 2E 6
Switchback Cl. SL6: Maid 2E 6
Switchback Rd. Nth. SL6: Maid 1F 7
Switchback Rd. Sth. SL6: Maid 2E 6
(not continuous)
Sycamore Cl. SL6: Maid 1D 12
(not continuous)
Sycamore Ct. SL4: Wind 2B 22
Sycamore Wlk. SL3: G Grn 5K 11
TW20: Eng G 5B 24
Sydney Gro. SL1: Slou 5B 10
Syke Cluan SL0: Rich P 1F 19
Syke Ings SL0: Rich P 2F 19
Sykes Rd. SL1: Slou 5A 10
Sylvester Rd. SL6: Maid 2F 7

T

Talbot Av. SL3: L'ly 1A 18
Talbot Ct. SL4: Wind 2A 22
Talbot Pl. SL3: Dat 7H 17
Talbots Dr. SL6: Maid 6C 6
Tall Trees SL3: Coln 7E 18
Tamarind Ct. TW20: Egh 4F 25
Tamarisk Way SL1: Slou 1K 15
Tamar Way SL3: L'ly 4C 18
Tangier Ct. SL4: Eton 5C 16
Tangier La. SL4: Eton 5C 16
Tapestries Hall SL4: Old Win 4F 23
TAPLOW 3B 8
Taplow Comn. Rd. SL1: Burn 1D 8
Taplow Quays SL6: Tap 5K 7
Taplow Rd. SL6: Tap 5D 8
Taplow Station (Rail) 5C 8
Tarbay La. SL4: Oak G 2E 20
Tarmac Way UB7: Harm 6J 19
Tatchbrook Cl. SL6: Maid 4H 7
Tavistock Cl. SL6: Maid 4B 6
Taylor's Bushes Ride SL4: Wind 7F 21
Taylors Ct. SL6: Maid 4C 6
Tectonic Pl. SL6: Holy 4J 13
Teesdale Rd. SL2: Slou 4J 9
Telford Dr. SL1: Slou 1K 15
Tempest Rd. TW20: Egh 5J 25
Temple Rd. SL4: Wind 1B 22
Temple Way SL2: Farn C 4E 4
Templewood Ga. SL2: Farn C 4E 4
Templewood La. SL2: Farn C, Stoke P 4E 4
Ten Acre La. TW20: Thorpe 7J 25
Tennyson Way SL2: Slou 3H 9

Terrace, The SL6: Bray . . . 2K **13**
Terrent Ct. SL4: Wind . . . 7K **15**
Testwood Rd. SL4: Wind . . . 7G **15**
Thames Av. SL4: Wind . . . 6C **16**
Thames Cres. SL6: Maid . . . 2J **7**
Thames Mead SL4: Wind . . . 7H **15**
Thames Rd. SL3: L'ly . . . 3B **18**
SL4: Wind . . . 6F **15**
Thames Side SL4: Wind . . . 6C **16**
Thames St. SL4: Wind . . . 7C **16**
THAMES VALLEY HOSPICE . . . 2K **21**
THAMES VALLEY NUFFIELD HOSPITAL . . . 7K **5**
Thames Valley University
Slough Campus . . . 7D **10**
Thatchers Dr. SL6: Maid . . . 7B **6**
Theatre Royal
Windsor . . . 6C **16**
Thicket Gro. SL6: Maid . . . 5A **6**
Third Cres. SL1: Slou . . . 4B **10**
Thirkleby Cl. SL1: Slou . . . 7B **10**
Thirlmere Av. SL1: Slou . . . 4F **9**
Thirlmere Cl. TW20: Egh . . . 6H **25**
Thompkins La. SL2: Farn R . . . 6B **4**
Thompson Cl. SL3: L'ly . . . 3B **18**
Thorncroft TW20: Eng G . . . 6C **24**
Thorndike SL2: Slou . . . 4K **9**
Thorn Dr. SL3: G Grn . . . 5K **11**
THORNEY . . . 2J **19**
Thorney Country Pk. . . . 2J **19**
Thorney La. Nth. SL0: Iver . . . 1G **19**
Thorney La. Sth. SL0: Rich P . . . 1G **19**
Thorney Mill Rd. SL0: Thorn . . . 2H **19**
(not continuous)
UB7: W Dray . . . 2H **19**
Thorpe By-Pass TW20: Thorpe . . . 7H **25**
Thorpe Ind. Pk. TW20: Thorpe . . . 7J **25**
THORPE LEA . . . 5J **25**
Thorpe Lea Rd. TW20: Egh, Thorpe . . . 5H **25**
Thorpe Rd. TW18: Staines . . . 5K **25**
Thrift La. SL6: Holy, Maid . . . 3D **12**
(not continuous)
Thurlby Way SL6: Maid . . . 2E **12**
Thurston Rd. SL1: Slou . . . 5D **10**
Tilbury Wlk. SL3: L'ly . . . 2C **18**
Tilstone Av. SL4: Eton W . . . 4H **15**
Tilstone Cl. SL4: Eton W . . . 4H **15**
Timbers Wlk. SL6: Maid . . . 7C **6**
Timberwood SL2: Farn C . . . 2F **5**
Tinkers La. SL4: Wind . . . 1G **21**
Tinsey Cl. TW20: Egh . . . 4H **25**
Tintern Cl. SL1: Slou . . . 2B **16**
Tiree Ho. SL2: Slou . . . 3A **10**
Tite Hill TW20: Egh, Eng G . . . 4D **24**
Tithe Barn Dr. SL6: Bray . . . 4A **14**
(not continuous)
Tithe Cl. SL6: Holy . . . 4K **13**
Tithe Ct. SL3: L'ly . . . 3B **18**
TITTLE ROW . . . 7C **6**
Tockley Rd. SL1: Burn . . . 2E **8**
Tollgate SL6: Maid . . . 6B **6**
Tomlin Rd. SL2: Slou . . . 3H **9**
Topaz Cl. SL1: Slou . . . 7A **10**
Torin Ct. TW20: Eng G . . . 4C **24**
Torquay Spur SL2: Slou . . . 2A **10**
Torridge Rd. SL3: L'ly . . . 5C **18**
TOUCHEN END . . . 7E **12**
Touchen End Rd. SL6: Holy . . . 7E **12**
Tourist Info. Cen.
Maidenhead . . . 5H **7**
Windsor . . . 7C **16**
Tower Ho. SL1: Slou . . . 1D **16**
Tower Ride SL4: Wind . . . 7H **21**
Town & Crown Exhibition . . . 7C **16**
Town Sq. SL1: Slou . . . 1E **16**
Tozer Wlk. SL4: Wind . . . 2G **21**
Tracy Av. SL3: L'ly . . . 4A **18**
Travic Rd. SL2: Slou . . . 2J **9**
Travis Ct. SL2: Farn R . . . 2A **10**
Treesmill Dr. SL6: Maid . . . 2C **12**
Trelawney Av. SL3: L'ly . . . 2J **17**
Trenchard Rd. SL6: Holy . . . 5J **13**
Trenches La. SL3: L'ly . . . 1B **18**
Trent Rd. SL3: L'ly . . . 5C **18**
Trent Vs. *SL3: Dat* . . . *7G* ***17***
(off Datchet Pl.)
Tressel, The SL6: Maid . . . 6E **6**
Trevelyan Ct. SL4: Wind . . . 1A **22**
Trevose Ho. *SL2: Slou* . . . *3A* ***10***
(off [illegible] Av.)
Trinity Pl. SL4: Wind . . . 1B **22**
Troutbeck Cl. SL2: Slou . . . 6F **11**
Trumper Way SL1: Slou . . . 7J **9**
Truro Cl. SL6: Maid . . . 5B **6**
Tubwell Rd. SL2: Stoke P . . . 7K **5**
Tudor Ct. SL6: Maid . . . 2K **7**
TW20: Egh . . . 4G **25**
Tudor Gdns. SL1: Slou . . . 5F **9**
Tudor La. SL4: Old Win . . . 6H **23**
Tudor Way SL4: Wind . . . 7H **15**
Tulip Way UB7: W Dray . . . 3K **19**
Tuns La. SL1: Slou . . . 2B **16**
Turks Head Ct. SL4: Eton . . . 6C **16**
Turner Rd. SL3: L'ly . . . 1H **17**
Turnoak Pk. SL4: Wind . . . 3H **21**
Turpins Grn. SL6: Maid . . . 7B **6**
Turton Way SL1: Slou . . . 2C **16**
Tweed Rd. SL3: L'ly . . . 5C **18**
Twinches La. SL1: Slou . . . 7A **10**
Two Mile Dr. SL1: Slou . . . 1H **15**
Twynham Rd. SL6: Maid . . . 5C **6**
Tyle Pl. SL4: Old Win . . . 4F **23**
Tyler Wlk. SL3: L'ly . . . 4A **18**
Tyrell Gdns. SL4: Wind . . . 2J **21**

U

UCI Cinema
Maidenhead . . . 6G **7**
Ullswater Cl. SL1: Slou . . . 4F **9**
Umberville Way SL2: Slou . . . 2J **9**
Underhill Cl. SL6: Maid . . . 6F **7**
Upcroft SL4: Wind . . . 2A **22**
Up. Bray Rd. SL6: Bray . . . 3K **13**
Up. Lees Rd. SL2: Slou . . . 2A **10**
UPTON . . . 2F **17**
Upton Cl. SL1: Slou . . . 2E **16**
Upton Ct. Rd. SL3: L'ly, Slou . . . 2F **17**
UPTON HOSPITAL . . . 1E **16**
Upton Lea Pde. SL2: Slou . . . 6G **11**
UPTON PARK . . . 2E **16**
Upton Pk. SL1: Slou . . . 2D **16**
Upton Rd. SL1: Slou . . . 2F **17**
Uxbridge Rd. SL1: Slou . . . 1F **17**
SL2: Slou . . . 1G **17**
SL3: G Grn, Wex . . . 4K **11**

V

Vale Gro. SL1: Slou . . . 2D **16**
Vale Rd. SL4: Wind . . . 6J **15**
Valley End SL3: Wex . . . 3H **11**
Vansittart Est. SL4: Wind . . . 6B **16**
Vansittart Rd. SL4: Wind . . . 7A **16**
Vantage Rd. SL1: Slou . . . 7A **10**
Vanwall Bus. Pk. SL6: Maid . . . 7D **6**
Vanwall Rd. SL6: Maid . . . 1D **12**
Vaughan Copse SL4: Eton . . . 3C **16**
Vaughan Gdns. SL4: Eton W . . . 3J **15**
Vaughan Way SL2: Slou . . . 3H **9**
Vauxhall Rd. SL6: Maid . . . 1D **12**
Vegal Cres. TW20: Eng G . . . 4B **24**
Verbena Cl. UB7: W Dray . . . 4K **19**
Verdon Ct. SL2: Farn R . . . 2A **10**
SL2: Slou . . . 2A **10**
Vermont Rd. SL2: Slou . . . 3J **9**
Verney Rd. SL3: L'ly . . . 3B **18**
Vicarage Av. TW20: Egh . . . 4H **25**
Vicarage Ct. TW20: Egh . . . 5H **25**
Vicarage Cres. TW20: Egh . . . 4H **25**
Vicarage Dr. SL6: Bray . . . 1K **13**
Vicarage Gdns. SL6: W Walt . . . 5A **12**
Vicarage La. TW19: Wray . . . 7K **23**
Vicarage Rd. SL6: Maid . . . 4G **7**
TW18: Staines . . . 2K **25**
TW20: Egh . . . 4G **25**
Vicarage Wlk. SL6: Bray . . . 1K **13**
Vicarage Way SL3: Coln . . . 6D **18**
Victor Cl. SL6: Maid . . . 4C **6**
Victoria Ct. *SL1: Slou* . . . *7D* ***10***
(off Blair Rd.)
Victoria Dr. SL1: Burn, Farn C . . . 5A **4**
SL2: Farn C . . . 5A **4**
Victoria Rd. SL2: Farn C . . . 5E **4**
SL2: Slou . . . 7G **11**
SL4: Eton W . . . 3H **15**
Victoria St. SL1: Slou . . . 1E **16**
SL4: Wind . . . 7C **16**
TW20: Eng G . . . 5C **24**
Victor Rd. SL4: Wind . . . 2B **22**
Village Rd. SL4: Dor . . . 2E **14**
Village Shop. Cen. *SL1: Slou* . . . *1E* ***16***
(off Buckingham Gdns.)
Villiers Ct. SL4: Wind . . . 6K **15**
Villiers Rd. SL2: Slou . . . 4C **10**
Vine Rd. SL2: Stoke P . . . 5H **5**
Viscount Ct. SL4: Wind . . . 7B **16**

W

Wade Dr. SL1: Slou . . . 7K **9**
Wagner Cl. SL6: Maid . . . 2A **12**
Wakefield Cres. SL2: Stoke P . . . 5H **5**
Waldeck Rd. SL6: Maid . . . 5H **7**
Walk, The SL4: Eton W . . . 4K **15**
Walker Ct. SL6: Maid . . . 5E **6**
Walker Cres. SL3: L'ly . . . 4A **18**
Walker Rd. SL6: Bray . . . 1H **13**
Wallace Wlk. SL3: Dat . . . 4E **16**
Wallis Ct. SL1: Slou . . . 1F **17**
Walnut Lodge SL1: Slou . . . 2C **16**
Walpole Rd. SL1: Slou . . . 5G **9**
SL4: Old Win . . . 6G **23**
Waltham Cl. SL6: Maid . . . 3A **12**
Waltham Rd. SL6: W Walt . . . 5A **12**
Walton La. SL2: Farn R . . . 1J **9**
Wapshott Rd. TW18: Staines . . . 5K **25**
Ward Gdns. SL1: Slou . . . 6H **9**
Ward Royal SL4: Wind . . . 7B **16**
Ward Royal Pde. *SL4: Wind* . . . *7B* ***16***
(off Alma Rd.)
Ward's Pl. TW20: Egh . . . 5J **25**
Warner Cl. SL1: Slou . . . 7H **9**
Warren Cl. SL3: L'ly . . . 2K **17**
Warren Ct. SL2: Farn C . . . 4E **4**
Warren Pde. SL2: Slou . . . 7H **11**
Warrington Av. SL1: Slou . . . 5B **10**
Warrington Spur SL4: Old Win . . . 6G **23**
Warwick Av. SL2: Slou . . . 3B **10**
TW20: Egh . . . 7J **25**
Warwick Cl. SL6: Maid . . . 2C **12**
Warwick Ct. *SL4: Wind* . . . *1B* ***22***
(off Alma Rd.)
Warwick Vs. TW20: Egh . . . 7J **25**
Washington Dr. SL1: Slou . . . 6G **9**
SL4: Wind . . . 2H **21**
Waterbeach Cl. SL1: Slou . . . 5C **10**
Waterbeach Rd. SL1: Slou . . . 5C **10**
Waterford Ho. UB7: W Dray . . . 2K **19**
Waterman Ct. SL1: Slou . . . 7H **9**
Watermans Bus. Pk. TW18: Staines . . . 3K **25**
WATER OAKLEY . . . 5C **14**
Waterside UB7: Harm . . . 6K **19**
Waterside Dr. SL3: L'ly . . . 1A **18**
Waters Reach SL6: Maid . . . 3H **7**
Wavell Gdns. SL2: Slou . . . 2J **9**
Wavell Rd. SL6: Maid . . . 6C **6**
Wavendene Av. TW20: Egh . . . 6H **25**
Waverley Rd. SL1: Slou . . . 4B **10**
Waylands TW19: Wray . . . 5K **23**
Wayside M. SL6: Maid . . . 4G **7**
Webb Cl. SL3: L'ly . . . 3J **17**
Webster Cl. SL6: Maid . . . 7B **6**
Weekes Dr. SL1: Slou . . . 7A **10**
Weint, The SL3: Coln . . . 6D **18**
Weirside Gdns. UB7: W Dray . . . 1K **19**
Welbeck Rd. SL6: Maid . . . 7E **6**
Welby Cl. SL6: Maid . . . 1B **12**
Welden SL2: Slou . . . 5H **11**
Welland Cl. SL3: L'ly . . . 5C **18**
Wellbank SL6: Tap . . . 3B **8**
Wellcroft Rd. SL1: Slou . . . 7A **10**
Wellesley Av. SL0: Rich P . . . 2G **19**
Wellesley Ct. SL0: Rich P . . . 1G **19**
Wellesley Ho. *SL4: Wind* . . . *7A* ***16***
(off Vansittart Rd.)
Wellesley Path *SL1: Slou* . . . *1F* ***17***
(off Wellesley Rd.)
Wellesley Rd. SL1: Slou . . . 7F **11**
Welley Av. TW19: Wray . . . 3K **23**
Welley Rd. SL3: Hort . . . 2K **23**
TW19: Wray . . . 5K **23**
Wellhouse Rd. SL6: Maid . . . 2F **7**
Wellington Lodge SL4: Wink . . . 7E **20**
Wellington Rd. SL6: Maid . . . 5E **6**
Wellington St. SL1: Slou . . . 7D **10**
Wells Cl. SL4: Wind . . . 7K **15**
Wendover Pl. TW18: Staines . . . 4K **25**
Wendover Rd. SL1: Burn . . . 4E **8**
TW18: Staines . . . 4J **25**
Wentworth Av. SL2: Slou . . . 1K **9**
Wentworth Cres. SL6: Maid . . . 6D **6**
Wentworth Ind. Ct. SL2: Slou . . . 2J **9**
Wesley Dr. TW20: Egh . . . 5G **25**
Wesley Pl. SL4: Wink . . . 7E **20**
Wessex Way SL6: Maid . . . 1C **12**
Westborough Ct. SL6: Maid . . . 6D **6**
Westborough Rd. SL6: Maid . . . 6D **6**
Westbrook SL6: Bray . . . 4B **14**
West Ct. SL6: Bray . . . 1K **13**
West Cres. SL4: Wind . . . 7J **15**
Westcroft SL2: Slou . . . 3A **10**
West Dean SL6: Maid . . . 4G **7**
WEST DRAYTON . . . 1K **19**
West End Ct. SL2: Stoke P . . . 7H **5**
West End La. SL2: Stoke P . . . 7G **5**
Western Perimeter Rd. TW6: H'row A . . . 7J **19**
UB7: Lford . . . 7J **19**
Westfield La. SL3: G Grn . . . 5J **11**
Westfield Rd. SL2: Slou . . . 3A **10**
SL6: Maid . . . 5C **6**
Westgate Cres. SL1: Slou . . . 6J **9**

Westgate Retail Pk. SL1: Slou 6K **9**
Westlands Av. SL1: Slou 5F **9**
Westlands Cl. SL1: Slou 5F **9**
Westmead SL4: Wind 2A **22**
SL6: Maid 2G **7**
Westmorland Rd. SL6: Maid 5E **6**
Weston Rd. SL1: Slou 4J **9**
West Point SL1: Slou 7G **9**
West Rd. SL6: Maid 5F **7**
West St. SL6: Maid 5G **7**
Wethered Dr. SL1: Burn 4E **8**
Wetton Pl. TW20: Egh 4F **25**
WEXHAM 3H 11
WEXHAM COURT 5H 11
WEXHAM PARK HOSPITAL 3H 11
Wexham Pk. La. SL3: Wex 3H **11**
Wexham Pk. Stadium 5F 11
Wexham Rd. SL1: Slou 1F **17**
SL2: Slou, Wex 5G **11**
WEXHAM STREET 1H 11
Wexham St. SL2: Wex 3G **11**
SL3: Stoke P 3G **11**
Wexham Woods SL3: Wex 4H **11**
Wharf Rd. TW19: Wray 6H **23**
Wheatbutts, The SL4: Eton W 3J **15**
Wheatfield Cl. SL6: Maid 1B **12**
Wheatlands Rd. SL3: Slou 2G **17**
Wheatsheaf Pde. *SL4: Old Win* *4F* ***23***
(off St Luke's Rd.)
Wheatstone Cl. SL3: Slou 2F **17**
Wheelwrights Pl. SL3: Coln 6D **18**
Whitby Rd. SL1: Slou 6B **10**
Whitby Rd. Bus. Cen. SL1: Slou 6B **10**
Whitchurch Cl. SL6: Maid 1F **7**
White Acres Dr. SL6: Holy 4K **13**
Whitebrook Pk. SL6: Maid 1K **7**
White Cl. SL1: Slou 7C **10**
Whiteford Rd. SL2: Slou 4D **10**
Whitehall Farm La. GU25: Vir W 7E **24**
(not continuous)
Whitehall La. TW20: Egh 6F **25**
White Hart Rd. SL1: Slou 2C **16**
Whitehart Rd. SL6: Maid 5G **7**
Whitehaven SL1: Slou 6E **10**
White Hermitage SL4: Old Win 4H **23**
White Horse Rd. SL4: Wind 2G **21**
Whitehouse Way SL3: L'ly 2J **17**
Whiteley SL4: Wind 6H **15**
White Lillies Island SL4: Wind 6K **15**
White Paddock SL6: Maid 3B **12**
White Rock SL6: Maid 3J **7**
Whites La. SL3: Dat 5G **17**
WHITE WALTHAM 5A 12
Whittaker Rd. SL2: Slou 3G **9**
Whittenham Cl. SL2: Slou 7F **11**
Whittle Parkway SL1: Slou 5G **9**
Whurley Way SL6: Maid 2F **7**
Wickets, The SL6: Maid 5D **6**
Wickham La. TW20: Egh 6G **25**
Wick La. TW20: Eng G 5A **24**
Wick Rd. TW20: Eng G 7A **24**
Widbrook Rd. SL6: Maid 1J **7**
Wiggington Ho. *SL4: Eton* *6C* ***16***
(off High St.)
Wildgreen Nth. SL3: L'ly 3B **18**
Wildgreen Sth. SL3: L'ly 3B **18**
Wilford Rd. SL3: L'ly 3K **17**
Willant Cl. SL6: Maid 3A **12**
William Ellis Cl. SL4: Old Win 4F **23**
William Hartley Yd. SL3: Wex 3G **11**
William St. SL1: Slou 1E **16**
SL4: Wind 7C **16**
Willoners SL2: Slou 4K **9**
Willoughby Rd. SL3: L'ly 2B **18**
Willowbrook SL4: Eton 3C **16**
Willow Cl. SL3: Coln 6D **18**
Willow Dr. SL6: Holy 3J **13**
Willow Pde. SL3: L'ly 2B **18**
Willow Pk. SL2: Stoke P 6J **5**
Willow Pl. SL4: Eton 5B **16**
Willows, The SL4: Wind 6G **15**
Willows Lodge SL4: Wind 6G **15**
Willows Path SL4: Wind 7F **15**
Willows Riverside Pk. SL4: Wind 6F **15**
Willow Wlk. TW20: Eng G 4C **24**
Willow Wood Cl. SL1: Burn 1E **8**
Willson Rd. TW20: Eng G 4B **24**
Wilmot Rd. SL1: Burn 2E **8**
Wilton Cres. SL4: Wind 3G **21**
Wiltshire Av. SL2: Slou 3B **10**
Winchester Cl. SL3: Poyle 7F **19**
Winchester Dr. SL6: Maid 2C **12**
Windermere Cl. TW20: Egh 6H **25**
Windermere Way SL1: Slou 4F **9**
Windmill Cl. SL4: Wind 1A **22**
Windmill Rd. SL1: Slou 7C **10**
Windmill Shott TW20: Egh 5F **25**
Windrush Av. SL3: L'ly 2C **18**
Windrush Way SL6: Maid 4G **7**
WINDSOR 7C 16
Windsor & Eton Central Station (Rail) 7C 16
Windsor & Eton FC 3A 22
Windsor & Eton Relief Rd.
SL4: Eton, Wind 7A **16**
Windsor & Eton Riverside Station (Rail) 6C 16
Windsor Boys School Sports Cen. 7A 16
Windsor Brass Rubbing Cen. *7C 16*
(off High St.)
Windsor Bus. Cen. SL4: Wind 6B **16**
Windsor Castle 6D 16
Windsor Cl. SL1: Burn 3F **9**
Windsor Fitness and Rackets Club, The 7A 16
Windsor La. SL1: Burn 3F **9**
Windsor Leisure Cen. 6A 16
Windsor Rd. SL1: Slou 2D **16**
SL2: Ger X, Stoke P 3J **5**
SL3: Dat 6F **17**
SL4: Old Win 7H **23**
SL4: Wat O, Wind 4A **14**
SL4: Wind 6E **14**
SL6: Bray 2H **13**
SL9: Ger X 1K **5**
TW19: Wray 5K **23**
TW20: Egh 7H **23**
Winkfield La. SL4: Wink 7A **20**
Winkfield Rd. SL4: Wink 7F **21**
Winston Ct. SL6: Maid 4C **6**
Winter Hill Rd. SL6: Maid 2B **6**
Wintoun Path SL2: Slou 3H **9**
Winvale SL1: Slou 2D **16**
Winwood SL2: Slou 5H **11**
SL4: Wind 7J **15**
Wise La. UB7: W Dray 2K **19**
Withey Cl. SL4: Wind 7H **15**
Withycroft SL3: G Grn 5K **11**
Wolf La. SL4: Wind 2G **21**
Wood Cl. SL4: Wind 3B **22**
Woodcote SL6: Maid 6E **6**
Wood End Cl. SL2: Farn C 2F **5**
Woodfield Dr. SL6: Maid 6B **6**
Woodford Way SL2: Slou 2K **9**
Woodhaw TW20: Egh 3H **25**
Woodhurst Nth. SL6: Maid 3K **7**
Woodhurst Rd. SL6: Maid 3J **7**
Woodhurst Sth. SL6: Maid 3K **7**
Woodland Av. SL1: Slou 6C **10**
SL4: Wind 3J **21**
Woodland Glade SL2: Farn C 2F **5**
Woodland Grange SL0: Rich P 2F **19**
Woodlands Bus. Pk. SL6: Maid 3B **12**
WOODLANDS PARK 3A 12
Woodlands Pk. Av. SL6: Maid 3B **12**
Woodlands Pk. Rd. SL6: Maid 3B **12**
Wood La. SL1: Slou 2J **15**
SL2: Hedg 1G **5**
Woodlee Cl. GU25: Vir W 7C **24**
Woods Dr. SL2: Farn C 4B **4**
Woodstock Av. SL3: L'ly 3J **17**
Woodstock Cl. SL6: Maid 3G **7**
WOOLLEY GREEN 7A 6
Wootton Way SL6: Maid 6D **6**
Worcester Cl. SL6: Maid 2D **12**
Worcester Gdns. SL1: Slou 1C **16**
Wordsworth Rd. SL2: Slou 3G **9**
WRAYSBURY 5K 23
Wraysbury Rd. TW18: Staines 2J **25**
TW19: Staines 1H **25**
Wren Ct. SL3: L'ly 2B **18**
Wren Dr. UB7: W Dray 2K **19**
Wright SL4: Wind 2F **21**
Wright Sq. SL4: Wind 2G **21**
Wright Way SL4: Wind 2F **21**
Wyatt Rd. SL4: Wind 2G **21**
Wylands Rd. SL3: L'ly 3B **18**
Wymers Cl. SL1: Burn 1E **8**
Wymer's Wood Rd. SL1: Burn 1D **8**
Wyndham Cres. SL1: Burn 1E **8**

Y

Yard Mead TW20: Egh 2G **25**
Yarmouth Rd. SL1: Slou 6B **10**
Ye Meads SL6: Tap 7B **8**
Yeoveney Cl. TW19: Staines 1K **25**
Yeovil Ent. Cen. SL2: Slou 4J **9**
Yeovil Rd. SL1: Slou 4H **9**
Yew Tree Cl. SL6: Maid 4F **7**
Yew Tree Rd. SL1: Slou 2F **17**
York Av. SL1: Slou 5B **10**
SL4: Wind 1A **22**
York Rd. SL4: Wind 1A **22**
SL6: Maid 6G **7**

The representation on the maps of a road, track or footpath is no evidence of the existence of a right of way.

The Grid on this map is the National Grid taken from Ordnance Survey mapping with the permission of the Controller of Her Majesty's Stationery Office.

Copyright of Geographers' A-Z Map Company Ltd.

No reproduction by any method whatsoever of any part of this publication is permitted without the prior consent of the copyright owners.